How
to
Succeed
in

# Winning
# Children
## TO Christ

**by George B. Eager**

Copyright © 1979 The Mailbox Club, Inc.

**The Mailbox Club**
**404 Eager Road**
**Valdosta, GA 31602**

Library of Congress Catalog Card No.: 79-92278

ISBN 0-9603752-0-1

Printed in United States of America
First printing November 1979
Second printing February 1982
Third printing October 1986
Fourth Printing July 1992

# CONTENTS

"I am convinced that there are thousands of people who could and would win children to Christ, if only someone would tell them what to do and how to do it."

George B. Eager

To LAURA,
my incredibly wonderful wife,
a true helpmeet from the Lord
and a constant joy and
encouragement to my heart.

WORDS OF GRATITUDE...To Doris Setliffe, Velma Mills, and Jackie McVey, my super-special co-workers, for their God-given wisdom and insight and for the many hours they spent helping me write and edit this book.

SPECIAL THANKS...To the Lowries— Jim, Marion, and Kathy, for their invaluable help in editing and layout.

GRATEFUL RECOGNITION...To Paul Labotz, now with the Lord, for all he taught me by example and precept.

"Here's one book you should not only own, but study and act upon if you really love children."

# INTRODUCTION E.V. THOMPSON
Chairman, WORLDTEAM

This book is a skillfully prepared guide for all who desire to be of spiritual and moral help to children. It presents in a most interesting and instructive fashion the way to lead children to an intelligent, growing faith in God and a living walk with Jesus Christ.

To develop this book required a deep understanding of child psychology, plus a knowledge and experience gained through teaching spiritual truths to children.

The author, George Eager, at the age of seven, had a real sense of spiritual need and went forward in an evangelistic meeting. Unfortunately, no one paid any attention to him or did anything to help him.

Years later, the accidental death of his seven-year-old son was the crushing blow that caused him to search out the reality of spiritual things. At the age of 32, he discovered real life through faith in Jesus Christ. He realized that he should have been guided to this truth as a child. As a result of this experience he became deeply concerned about the spiritual needs of children.

Through the leading of the Holy Spirit, George and Laura Eager committed themselves to the great task of winning children to Christ. During the following twenty years, he conducted over

3,700 meetings for children and young people. Thousands were led to the Lord.

God richly blessed these meetings, but George Eager was deeply concerned about following up those who had made decisions—to guide them to spiritual maturity. He has developed several series of Bible correspondence lessons which are spiritual gems—simple, clearly explained and wonderfully illustrated.

Through the concept of individually or group operated Mailbox Clubs, thousands of God's people have joined George Eager's efforts and multiplied the far-reaching ministry of this program. Today, millions of Mailbox Club lessons are printed each year for distribution in this country and others.

In the book you will notice how, step-by-step, the author points out and illustrates successful ways of leading children from active sin and spiritual death to repentance and conscious faith in the Lord Jesus Christ. The author's emphasis on the important place of the cross of Christ in Christian teaching is very pertinent.

The section that teaches and demonstrates that saved children and teen-agers can be led to victory and lead consistent Christian lives through faith in Christ is one of the most significent features of this book.

I pray and trust that this book will be thankfully received, carefully read, and its principles faithfully applied by God's people all over the world.

Elmer V. Thompson, Chairman
WORLDTEAM

# AUTHOR'S PREFACE

Some time ago a young lady wrote asking about an object lesson I use in children's meetings. She had been introduced to this particular object lesson as a fourth grader when she attended one of my presentations. It made a lasting impression on her. She now wanted to use it in teaching her Sunday school class.

The requested materials were sent to her along with suggestions for their use. Some time later I received another letter from her expressing great excitement. She wrote, "I taught 6th grade VBS at our church last week, and on Wednesday, after using the heart illustration, seven people received Christ. On Thursday we had several decisions in the joint assembly, and on Friday, during our class, we had three more receive Christ. You can imagine my excitement!"

I got excited too. I thought, "There must be thousands of people like this friend — people who could and would win children to Christ, if only someone would tell them what to do and how to do it."

Hence this book. My object has been to share with other believers practical information that would enable them to evangelize children and to lead them into victorious, fruitful Christian lives.

My prayer is that God will use this book to open your eyes to see the multitude of lost children and to inspire you to get started in the greatest work in all the world — winning children to Christ.

George B. Eager

How
to
Succeed
in

# Winning
# Children
## TO Christ

**by George B. Eager**

Published by
Mailbox Club Books
404 Eager Road
Valdosta, Georgia 31602

Layout and Illustrations
James R. Lowrie

Cover
Diana Philbrook

# Part One

## Why Evangelize Children?

**Christian workers have the never-ending job of telling others that the Son of God died for them that they might be saved.**

"When a boy or girl thrusts his small hand into yours, it may be smeared with chocolate ice cream, or grimy from petting a dog. There may be a wart under the right thumb and a bandage around the little finger. But the important thing about his hand is that it is the hand that some day may hold a Bible or a Colt revolver; play a piano or spin a gambling wheel; gently dress a leper's wound or tremble wretchedly, uncontrolled by an alcoholic mind. Right now, that hand is yours...it asks for help and guidance."

*Author unknown*

# The World's
# *Most Fruitful*
# Mission
# Field

**The world's most fruitful mission field
is not a particular place.
It is not a particular country.
It's a certain kind of people—it's children!**

No group of people is more open to the gospel.
No group responds so warmly and wholeheartedly.
And children are everywhere!

Lionel Hunt records these statistics in his book,
*Handbook of Children's Evangelism:*

**86%** |← 86% are saved before reaching →|
15 years of age.

**10%** ←→ Only 10% are saved between
15 and 30 years of age.

**4%** |←  A scant 4% are saved after 30.

The great evangelist, D.L. Moody, was returning
from a meeting one day when someone asked,

"How many souls were saved at the meeting?"

"Two and a half," said Mr. Moody.

"Two adults and one child?" inquired the man.

"No," replied Mr. Moody, "two children and one adult!"

This man of God, one of the greatest evangelists of all time, saw the importance of winning children to Christ. When a child is saved, not only is a soul saved, but a life as well. Someone said, "Save an adult and you save a unit; save a child and you save a multiplication table."

R. A. Torrey said, "It is almost the easiest thing in the world to lead a child from five to ten years of age to a definite acceptance of Christ...The younger the children are when you seek to lead them to make an actual acceptance of Christ, the easier the work will be, and the more satisfactory."

That prince of preachers, Charles Spurgeon, said, "A child of five, if properly instructed, can as readily believe and be regenerated as anyone."

More than forty years ago, a pastor named Irvin Overholtzer was challenged by Spurgeon's statement. He put it to the test and found that it worked! He found that children, even very young children, readily came to the Lord, and their lives subsequently proved that their conversions were real.

God so stirred Mr. Overholtzer's heart that he gave his life to the work of winning children. He founded Child Evangelism Fellowship, a world-wide organization with over 600 full-time workers and over 60,000 volunteer helpers.

The fact that children can be saved should not be surprising to us. Indeed, to "become as little children" is a prime condition for entering the kingdom of Heaven. The Lord Jesus said, "Except you be converted, and become as little children, you shall not enter into the kingdom of heaven."

Children really have an advantage over adults since they are already "little children." Their hearts are naturally open. They are honest and sincere. Their hearts are tender. When you point out their sins to them, they are deeply moved and readily admit their sins.

Faith comes easily to children. Isaac Watts was saved at the age of 9, Jonathan Edwards at 7, Matthew Henry at 11, Jim Elliot at 6, and Henrietta Mears, Corrie Ten Boom, and Ruth Graham at 5 years of age.

> **"It is not the will of your Father which is in heaven, that one of these little ones should perish."** Jesus Christ

We often hear a parent say, "I want my child to wait to receive Christ until he is old enough to know what he is doing." Children *should* know what they are doing when they come to Christ. But if children are old enough to know that they have sinned, they are old enough to know that they need a Savior.

Jesus said, "Take heed that you despise not one of these little ones." Putting it positively, He is saying, "Treasure children, pay attention to them, take them seriously." Unfortunately, we do not always do this. One of my earliest childhood recollections is that of going forward at the conclusion of a series of evangelistic meetings at our church. I was about seven years old at the time, and I was deeply concerned about my sins.

As I headed down to the altar from the balcony, I thought everybody would come to accept this salvation that was being offered. But, as it turned out, I was the only one!

Unfortunately, no one took this small boy seriously. The evangelist, the pastor, and the elders came by and shook my hand or patted me on the head. But no one took me aside and showed me from God's Word how I could be saved and know it. I went home and wept bitterly, but I was not saved. It was twenty-five years later, after the death of our 7-year-old son, that I was truly born again.

### Some may not take children seriously, but our Lord did!

The Scriptures record an instance when young children were being brought to Jesus for His blessing. The disciples took it upon themselves to restrain and rebuke those who brought the children. When Jesus saw this, He was moved with indignation and said, "Suffer the little children to come unto Me, and forbid them not: for of such is the kingdom of God."

A little girl was trying to quote this verse before an audience but she was struck with stage fright.

She stammered, "Jesus said, 'Suffer...Suffer...'" Jesus wants all of us to come to Him and don't anybody try to stop us!" Jesus *does* want all children to come to Him, but before they can, they must hear about Him. It's our job to tell them!

We think most everybody knows about Coke; yet the Coca-Cola Company spends millions of dollars each year advertising their product. Do you wonder why they do this?

An executive with the company explained it: "Each year several hundred million people die. They are no longer customers for Coca-Cola. Each year, several hundred million people are born. They have never heard about Coca-Cola. We have a never-ending job of telling these people about our product."

We Christians have the most wonderful "product" in all the world, but people must hear about it. Each year, millions of children are born into this world. They know nothing about Jesus Christ and His salvation. Christian workers have the never-ending job of telling children everywhere that God loves them and that Jesus died for them that they might belong to Him eternally.

# 2

# Who Can Win Children?

Be an
☑ **Effective**
CHILDREN'S
WORKER

*Happy is the person
God calls to
work with children*

The apostolic church carried the gospel to the entire known world in approximately 33 years. How did they do it? They simply followed God's plan. What is God's plan for evangelizing the world? It is this—every believer telling someone the story of Jesus, not only with his lips but also with his life. Happy is the person whom God calls to the work of evangelizing children.

Who can win children to Christ? Any believer! Adults can win children, teen-agers can win children, and children can win children. And no work is more exciting and fruitful.

A children's worker impressed this on me one day in a church service. He was speaking about the verse in which Jesus said, "Follow Me, and I will make you fishers of men." Holding his hands out wide, he asked, "How many of you have ever caught a fish this big?" No hands went up. He brought his hands closer together and asked, "How many of you have ever caught a fish this big?" A few hands went up. Then he brought his hands close together, only a few inches apart, and asked, "How many of you have ever caught a fish *this* big?" Almost every hand went up! Then he made his point: "Children are 'little fish.' You can catch them for Christ so easily."

How true! Any believer who loves the Lord and loves souls can win children to Christ. To be effective, a children's worker should:

- **Love children** and believe that they are important.

- Realize that **every child has infinite possibilities** and treat each one as a Very Important Person.

- See that, **without Christ, the child is lost** and "dead in trespasses and sins"; see that every unsaved child needs to be "born again" through faith in Jesus Christ.

- Believe that **children can be saved;** believe that they can understand the essentials of the gospel.

- **Learn to speak to children** on their level of understanding and seek ways of making the gospel plain to them.

- **Learn new ways** of catching and holding children's attention when presenting the gospel, making the message entertaining as well as enlightening. No one should bore children with a dull and uninteresting message.

● **Be enthusiastic!** Enthusiasm is the highest priced commodity in the business world. Enthusiastic leaders and salesmen are much sought after. We have something far better than anything this world has to offer. Let's be enthusiastic about it!

● **Expect results.** A young preacher was discouraged and he went to an older pastor for counsel. The pastor asked, "Do you expect someone to be saved every time you preach?" "Oh, no," replied the young man. "I don't expect that!" "Then perhaps that is why you are not winning souls," said the pastor.

A. B. Simpson said, "The success of some evangelists is all out of proportion to their talent or capability, but they have one gift which they faithfully exercise and that is expecting God to give them souls, and therefore they are never disappointed."

● **Be filled with "the joy of the Lord."** Children are attracted to those whose hearts overflow with contagious joy. If they see we have something so good that we can't keep it to ourselves, they will want it. In winning children to Christ, a pound of joy is worth a ton of logic!

---

**"Children are 'little fish.' You can catch them for Christ so easily."** Paul LaBotz

---

D. L. Moody recognized the importance of children and never slighted them in his meetings. Once an usher kept a little boy from attending one of Moody's services in Denver, Colorado, because there were no seats left. The little boy sat down on the steps in front of the church and began weeping. Moody came by and asked the boy why he was crying. When the boy told him, Moody told the little boy to hang on to his coattails. He led him through the crowd right up to the platform. Moody explained to the audience, "This boy was crying because he was told there was no place for him to sit. Well, I want him here, so I've given him a place on the platform. Pray that he will turn out to be the best boy in America!" A loud "Amen" came from the crowd. Much impressed by Moody's love and concern, the little boy listened to every word of the message. When he grew up he became a prominent evangelist himself, leading thousands to Christ. His name—Paul Rader!

> "If I deal with twenty adults, I am usually able to lead one to Christ. But if I deal with twenty children, nineteen of them will accept Christ...If I had my life to live over, I would devote it to child evangelism." *Dr. Paul Rood*

# 3

# What Is
# the Gospel?

The gospel of
Christ is "the
power of
God unto
salvation."
Romans 1:16

Unsaved children cannot be brought into
the Kingdom of God by giving them a
pep talk on "How to be better boys and
girls," or by exhorting them to be
baptized or to join a church. They
must be "born again."

In order for children to be born again, they
must hear and believe the gospel. The Bible says
that the gospel of Christ is "the power of God
unto salvation to every one that believeth."

The word "gospel" means "good news," but
many people do not understand what this good
news is. The "good news" is not that God loves
only good people and saves only those who always
do His will. This would not be good news at all to
us, for we are all sinners.

The "good news" of the gospel is that God loves sinners and rebels such as you and I, and that He gave His Son to die for us that we might be reconciled to Him.

Paul stated the gospel so simply that a small child can easily understand it:

**"I declare unto you the gospel...**
    **that Christ *died* for our sins**
        **according to the Scriptures;**
           **And that He was *buried*,**
                **And that He *rose again* the third day**
                **according to the Scriptures."**

From these verses we see that the gospel of Jesus Christ rests on two great facts:
    (1) Christ died for our sins.
    (2) Christ rose from the dead.

Actually, the Bible tells us about a number of people whom God raised from the dead. In every instance, however, these people died later on. But with the Lord Jesus it was different. He rose from the grave, never to die again. He said, "I am He that liveth, and was dead; and, behold, I am alive forevermore."

Where did Paul get this gospel which he preached? He got it from the risen Christ Himself! It cannot be emphasized too strongly that the gospel taught by Paul in his epistles is the Lord's own explanation of His death and resurrection. Paul said, "I certify you, brethren, that the gospel which was preached of me is not after man. For I neither received it of man, neither was I taught it, but by the revelation of Jesus Christ."

A child must believe the gospel in order to be saved, and he cannot believe it unless he hears it. It is sad but true that a child may attend Sunday school and church faithfully for years and not hear the simple gospel. Very few children know the gospel! You can verify this by simply asking a number of children how a person can be saved. The vast majority will say, "By being good," or something similar. Some believe a person is saved by being baptized or by joining the church.

How blessed it is to be able to tell children the wonderful "good news"—that God loves them, that Jesus died for their sins, and that they can be saved the moment they trust Him as their Savior.

Our purpose in giving the gospel to children is this: to show them that they need a Savior, and that the Lord Jesus is the very Savior they need.

Irvin Overholtzer, the founder of Child Evan-

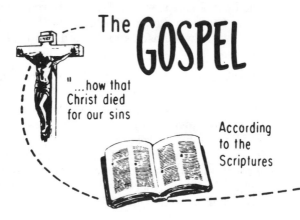

The **GOSPEL**

"...how that Christ died for our sins

According to the Scriptures

gelism Fellowship, relates this conversation with a child:

> I asked a little girl of ten whether she was a Christian. She answered that she did not know. I asked her whether she was saved. Again she did not know. I asked her, "How do we get saved?" She answered, "By being good." I said, "How good do you have to be?" She answered, "Awful good." "How awful good?" I asked. "Awful, awful good," she replied. I said, "Are you that good?" She said that she was not. I said, "Well, I guess you are not saved then." Then I said, "I am not that good either." She had known me as the minister in her community. I shall never forget how big her eyes became as she looked at me, as much as to say, "Well, if you are not that good, then you are not saved. And if you are the preacher and you are not saved, pray then who is saved?" Then with great earnestness she asked,

And that
He was buried,

And that He rose
again the third day...."

I. Corinthians 15:3,4

"How then do you get saved?" What a joy it was to explain God's plan of salvation through the finished work of Christ on the cross. She accepted the Lord so readily and then she was sure she was saved. That was nine years ago... She is nineteen now and is still standing fast in the Lord.[1]

When we give children the gospel in the power of God's Holy Spirit, we will see results. The gospel is indeed "the power of God unto salvation to every one that believeth."

# Why Couldn't God Just Forgive Us?

Why did
Jesus have
to die?

The Apostle Paul said that the message of the Cross—that Christ died for our sins and rose again —is "the wisdom of God." It reveals God's infinite wisdom as to the only way man can be redeemed and brought back into fellowship with his Creator.

> In giving the gospel to children, we must help them to understand:
> (1) The purpose of Christ's death.
> (2) The necessity of His death.

## The Purpose of Christ's Death

Christ died on a Roman cross—that is a fact of history. But the important thing is *why* He died. God left no room for doubt as to the purpose of Christ's death. He died for our sins. The Holy Spirit, through the prophet Isaiah, wrote:

"He hath borne OUR griefs,
and carried OUR sorrows...
He was wounded for OUR transgressions,
He was bruised for OUR iniquities:
the chastisement of OUR peace was
upon Him;
and with HIS STRIPES we are
healed."

Today, many in the religious world preach that Christ died for a good cause, or that He died to show us how we must face suffering and death courageously. But this is *not* why Christ died. He died as the Lamb of God, shedding His blood for our sins. The Lord Jesus said, "This is my blood... which is shed for many for the remission of sins."

It is very important that children get a right concept of the Cross. The Cross is not God laying our sins on an innocent, third party. This concept caused one little girl to say, "I love Jesus, but I hate God."

No, a thousand times no! God is not a "meany" in Heaven, while Jesus is so loving and kind that He came to earth to die for us. The true meaning of the Cross is God Himself taking our punishment and dying for our sins. Jesus Christ *is God* —"For in Him dwelleth all the fullness of the Godhead bodily."

Amazing love! How can it be
That Thou, my God, shouldest die for me?

## The Necessity of Christ's Death

The death of Christ on the cross was absolutely

necessary for two good reasons: (1) to meet the sinner's needs, and (2) to provide a way whereby God could forgive us righteously.

**1. The Cross meets the sinner's needs.** The Bible says, "It is the blood that makes an atonement for the soul." There is no divine forgiveness apart from the shedding of blood. Hebrews 9:22 says, "Without the shedding of blood there is no forgiveness."

Yes, but whose blood? Could I die for your sins? No, because I, too, am a sinner. It took nothing less than the death of God's Son to atone for our sins. The Bible says, "Ye were not redeemed with corruptible things, as silver and gold...but with the precious blood of Christ, as of a lamb without blemish and without spot."

Because the Son of God died for my sins, I know they are forgiven. The Bible says,"...we have redemption through His blood, the forgiveness of sins." I do not have to fear God. I can come boldly into His presence. "Having therefore, brethren, boldness to enter into the holiest by the blood of Jesus..."

**2. The Cross satisfies God's righteousness.** It provides the means by which God can be "just and Justifier of him that believes in Jesus."

Many children (and adults) do not understand why Jesus had to die on the cross. They ask, "Why couldn't God just forgive us? Why did Jesus have to die?"

The reason God could not "just forgive us"

is that He is the righteous Judge of the universe, and we have broken His laws. He has said, "The soul that sinneth, it shall die." And God must uphold His holy laws.

We have sinned; therefore, we deserve to perish. God loves us and wants to save us; yet He cannot be unrighteous. The Bible says, "The Lord is righteous in all His ways..."

God cannot overlook our sins or pretend that He does not know about them. Whatever God does must be in accord with *all* His attributes, including His righteousness and His justice.

How did God provide salvation for us and yet maintain His righteousness? He did it through the Cross. The Cross is the price God paid to redeem us.

> God could not pass the sinner by;
>> his sin demands that he should die.
> But in the cross of Christ we see
>> how God could save and righteous be!
>>>> Denham Smith

The huge LaGuardia International Airport is named after a former mayor of New York, Fiorello LaGuardia. He was loved and admired by people of all political parties.

Once, when Mr. LaGuardia was a city judge, an old man was brought into the court, charged with stealing a loaf of bread. The man admitted his guilt, but said that he was hungry.

Judge LaGuardia was sympathetic. He said, "I am sorry that you had to steal to satisfy your hunger, but we cannot allow people to steal.

The law says that you must pay a fine or you must go to jail. As your judge, I must carry out the law. I fine you ten dollars."

The man looked down and shook his head saying, "I have no money. I cannot pay the fine."

Then Judge LaGuardia did a wonderful thing. He took off his judicial robes and came down to where the man was standing. Placing his hand upon the man's shoulder, he said, "As your judge, I had to sentence you. As your friend, I want to pay your fine for you." He reached into his pocket, took out a ten dollar bill, and paid the man's fine.

We are like the man who could not pay. We have broken God's laws and deserve eternal punishment. But our Lord laid aside His glory and came to earth and paid the penalty of our sins on the Cross.

The Cross shows us God's love. It also reveals His righteousness. The Bible says, "For therein is the righteousness of God revealed." Because Christ paid the just penalty of our sins, God can *righteously* forgive the person who trusts Christ as his Savior.

We now see the place that the Cross has in salvation. It is absolutely essential. Without the Cross no one could be saved. With the Cross anyone can be saved, and that includes children!

We need never fear telling children about Christ's death on the cross as long as we show them God's love in it and tell them how they can appropriate its benefits.

The Cross has always been in the mind and heart of God. Jesus Christ is "the Lamb slain from the foundation of the world." In Heaven there is an eternal glorying in Christ's great sacrifice. The millions upon millions who gather around the throne sing praises to Him saying, "Thou art worthy...for Thou wast slain, and hast redeemed us to God by Thy blood."

# 5

# Repentance

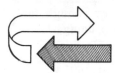

## The Vital TURN-AROUND

**Salvation is more than just
believing the facts of the Gospel!**

**God's redemption is perfect and complete**...but
this does not automatically save anyone. There
must be a response on our part.

Salvation is more than just believing the facts
of the gospel. It involves being sorry for sin,
turning from sin, and trusting in Jesus Christ.
The Bible calls this "repentance toward God, and
faith toward our Lord Jesus Christ."

It is said that, out of 100 children who are
"taken" to church at early ages, only 10 continue
in attendance by the time they reach adulthood.
One reason for this may be that most of those who
drop out were never saved. We can take children
to Sunday school and church, but if they are not
born again, they will have no real interest in
spiritual things. And, as soon as they are old
enough to go their own way, they will leave.

We live in a day of "easy believism." It is easy to get children to hold up their hands to indicate a decision, but that does not mean they are saved. The Bible says that no one can be saved unless he repents. Jesus said plainly, "Except ye repent, ye shall all likewise perish."

> **Repentance is being sorry enough for your sins to want to stop doing them.**

What does it mean to repent, and why is this necessary to salvation? Repentance is not just being sorry for one's sins. Judas was sorry that he betrayed the Lord, but he did not repent. Repentance is not conviction alone. A person may be convicted of his sins, and yet not repent.

What then, is repentance? Here is a simple definition: *Repentance is being sorry enough for your sins to want to stop doing them.* Even small children can understand this.

When a person sincerely changes his heart attitude, a change in his actions will follow. David expressed it well when he·said, "I thought on my ways, and turned my feet unto Thy testimonies."

There is a reason why a person must repent before he can be saved. God's objective is a kingdom for His Son. He has ordained that Jesus Christ shall reign forever. The Bible says, "For to this end Christ both died, and rose...that He might be Lord..." This presents a problem for us because we are "born rebels." The Bible says, "We have turned every one to his own way." We don't want anybody telling us what to do—not even God Himself!

Can a person be forgiven of his sins and brought into Christ's kingdom while he is still a rebel at heart? No, he cannot. There are no rebels in "the kingdom of God's dear Son."

If we want to enter Christ's kingdom, there must be a fundamental change inside of us. Self must be dethroned, and Christ must be enthroned. Our wills must be submitted to Him.

We must help children to understand the root of their sin problem and show them what to do about it. Our sins are many, but the *root* of the problem is self-will—wanting to have our own way.

The remedy is turning from sin and self to Christ. He can deliver us from our sins—that is the very thing He came to do. The Lord Jesus did not come simply to save us from eternal punishment. He came to save us from our sins! "Thou shalt call His name JESUS: for He shall save His people from their sins."

We cannot insist that children give up their sins before they can be saved, but they must be willing to give them up. We must impress on them the necessity of being truly sorry for their sins— sorry enough to want to turn from them.

What a joy it is when there is true conviction of sin and evidence of real repentance! One little girl came to me after a meeting and said, "I've asked Jesus to come into my heart, and I'm going to do my *very best* not to sin any more!" Another wrote to me, "I have come to my senses. I have been saying bad words and I was not obeying my mother right sometimes. You have made a new life for me. I have stopped doing these things when I heard you."

To bring children to repentance, they must first be convicted of their sins. Children must know that they are sinners, and that they need a savior. The Holy Spirit brings conviction as we tell them of God's holy laws. "For by the law is the knowledge of sin."

The Bible makes it clear that no one can be saved by keeping the law; nevertheless, the law has a vital function in bringing a person to Christ. The law shows a person that he is a sinner, that he is condemned, and that he needs a savior. Paul said that the law is a "schoolmaster to bring us to Christ, that we might be justified by faith."

If you want to see children come to Christ, explain God's holy laws to them, especially the Ten Commandments. Trust the Holy Spirit to work in their hearts as you spell out what sin is. Then tell them of the Savior who died for them.

For many years now at our summer camp, I have been able to predict quite accurately the night when most unsaved children will come to Christ. It is the night I speak on the Ten Commandments. (In preparation for this message, I like to read D.L. Moody's book, *Weighed and Found Wanting* —Moody Press.)

Some time ago I received a letter from a seven-year-old boy. It was a masterpiece of simplicity and directness. He wrote, "Dear Mr. Eager, I want

you to come back. And I learned not to steal.
Love, Dwayne."

**We should know and teach the following aspects
of sin:**

# SIN HURTS US

Because of our sins we are separated from God
and condemned to death. The Bible says, "The
wages of sin is death."

Fear of punishment is not the highest motiva-
tion for coming to Christ, but it is a powerful one,
and one that must not be disregarded. God has
said that He will judge sin, and we do well to
warn children in a loving way of the consequences
of rejecting God's gracious offer of salvation.

# SIN HURTS OTHERS

Which of us has not felt the pangs of guilt as
we contemplated the sorrow and distress that our
sins have caused others? Often, when everything
else has failed, the remembrance of a mother's
tears has brought a wayward son back to the Lord.

# SIN HURTS GOD

Children need to know this: *Sin hurts God's
heart.* We have broken God's laws, but more than
that, we have broken His heart. In dealing with
children, I have found this to be the deepest and
most convicting aspect of sin.

 We all know the story of the Prodigal Son. For the most part, our attention is on the son. But the very essence of the story is the father and his great love. This is but a faint picture of God's love for His "prodigal sons." The realization of how much we have sinned against His great love is most powerful in moving us to repentance.

After one of my meetings, three girls came to talk with me. One of them said, "Mr. Eager, we would like to talk to you a few minutes." I said, "Fine. What would you like to talk to me about?" Tears began to flow as she said, "I've been cussin' and saying a lot of dirty words. I thought it was kinda smart, but now I see God hates it, and I want to ask the Lord to forgive me." The other girls said the same thing, and all three came to Christ that day.

At my next meeting I related the incident. Afterward, as I started to my car, four girls came to speak to me, and one said, "We are just like those three girls except there are four of us."

Ever since this incident, I have told about the three girls in my message. Many, many children —even small children—have come to see me after the meetings confessing that they, too, were guilty of this sin of bad talk.

Through this experience I discovered a valuable principle: Telling what *other* children have confessed to you as sin is one of the best ways of showing children their sins. Children relate to these stories and the Holy Spirit shows them that they, too, are guilty of the same sins.

Sometimes children confess unusual sins, but no matter what sin a child confesses to you, always seek to understand. Never, never laugh at him.

> **Telling what other children have con-fessed as sin is one of the best ways of showing children their sins.**

At one meeting a little girl confessed to me the sin of breaking her glasses. She said, "I broke my glasses eleven times, but I'm not going to do it any more!"

In amazement I asked, "You broke your glasses eleven times? How did you do that?"

"I threw them down on the pavement and broke them."

"Why did you do that?" I inquired.

"Because everybody calls me 'Four Eyes.' But now I've taken Jesus as my Savior, and I'm not going to break them any more."

This girl's outward sin was breaking her glasses, but the deep, inner sins were pride, resentment, and anger. When she repented, her inner attitude changed, and there was a corresponding change in her outward actions.

Repentance is essential to salvation. We cannot by-pass it. The Bible says, "God...now commands all men everywhere to repent."

A. W. Tozer said, "Millions try to believe without having first repented. They try to have faith without intending to bring their lives into moral conformity with the law of God. Repent and believe is the order. Faith will follow repentance, and salvation will be the outcome."

At one of James Stewart's evangelistic meetings in Scotland, he invited the listening crowd to come forward to accept a copy of the Gospel of John if they were interested in being saved. Immediately, a young girl of fourteen came forward. He asked, "Why do you want to accept Christ as your Savior? Why do you want to be saved?" The answer came back clear as crystal, "Please sir, I do not want to live a life of sin." A better answer could not have been given.

# 6

# What Is Saving Faith?

When a child sees that he is a sinner and wants to turn from his sins, he will receive with joy the wonderful news that the Lord Jesus will save him. Here is where saving faith comes in.

What is saving faith?

**Saving faith is faith in the person and work of Jesus Christ.**

This faith brings us into a living relationship with the living Savior. The Bible says, "We are made partakers of Christ..." God is not interested in just changing our outward behavior. He wants to bring us into a living relationship with His Son. This is salvation!

How does a person come into this vital relationship with Jesus Christ? By *believing* and *receiving*. The Bible says, "Believe on the Lord Jesus Christ" (Acts 16:31), and "receive Him" (John 1:12).

What does it mean to "believe" on Him and "receive" Him?

## Believe on the Lord Jesus Christ.

There is only one place in the Bible where the question "What must I do to be saved?" is asked directly. The answer which Paul gives to this question is: "Believe on the Lord Jesus Christ and you shall be saved..." To understand what it means to believe on Him, we need to know the meaning of His name.

"**LORD**" — This is His kingly name that stands for His rulership over all things. He has all power in Heaven and earth. He is "Lord of all." To believe on Him as Lord means to take Him as your Master and to obey Him.

"**JESUS**" — This is His personal, human name. It means "Savior." Jesus died on the cross to save us from the *penalty* of our sins. He lives in us to save us from the *power* of sin. And one day He is coming back to take us to be with Him, where we shall forever be saved from the *presence* of sin.

"**CHRIST**" — This is His official name. It means "the anointed One." He is God's anointed King. The Bible says that God has made Him to be "both Lord and Christ."

## Receive Him.

To be saved, a person must not only believe that Christ died for his sins, but he must also receive

Him as his personal Savior. Ruth Paxson used to say, "To become a child of God, there is something to *believe* and Someone to *receive*."

# SALVATION
## THRU JESUS CHRIST
*God's Free Gift*

We receive the gift of eternal life when we receive the Lord Jesus as our Savior.

## Salvation is a Person— The Lord Jesus Christ!

God has given Him to us to be our Savior. John 3:16 says, "For God so loved the world, that He *gave* His only begotten Son..."

But we must receive Him in order for Him to be our Savior. John 1:12 says, "As many as *received* Him, to them gave He power to become the sons of God..."

## What does it mean to "receive Christ"?

To receive Christ means to take Him as your Savior and to follow Him. Jesus said, "My sheep hear My voice, and I know them, and they follow Me."

Children know what it means to follow a "bully," and they know what it is to "follow the crowd." We want to show them how much better it is to follow Christ.

We must present Christ in His resurrection power. He is the glorious, risen Christ who conquered sin and death. He has all power in Heaven and in earth.

He is the reigning Lord...
over Heaven? Yes!
over earth? Yes!
over death? Yes!
over sin? Indeed, Yes!

Christ is Lord of ALL! And if He is Lord of all, then He is worthy to be followed, worshipped, and served.

**To receive Christ means to take Him as your Savior and to follow Him.**

## SALVATION—A gift received by faith

The idea that salvation is "earned" by being good is thoroughly ingrained in children. Nearly all children think that salvation is by works. To correct this, we must show them that salvation is a GIFT. The "gift" is the Lord Jesus Himself. God has given this glorious, risen Christ to us to be our Savior.

The gift idea is very appealing to children. It shows them that salvation is free, that it must be received, that it can be taken instantly, and that it is theirs as soon as they take it.

John 3:16 is excellent for explaining the gift aspect of salvation, especially when the truth is illustrated. Here is the way I explain it to a group of children:

Now I'm going to say a very familiar verse. I'm going to say part of the verse and I'm going to let you say part. *(Pause at the blank places and let the children supply the words.)*

"For God so loved the ——————that He gave His only begotten ——————that whosoever believeth in Him should not ——————. but have —————— ————."

Whom does God mean when He says "the world"? He means all of us. We are in the world. And this verse says that whosoever believes in Him shall not perish but have everlasting life. To "perish" means to be lost, to be separated from God forever. God does not want any of us to perish.

What did God give to us? He gave His Son! This means that He gave the Lord Jesus to us to be our Savior. He gave Jesus to die on the cross for our sins.

Why did God give us a Savior? Because we needed one! We have all said wrong things. We have all done wrong things. We cannot go to Heaven with sin in our hearts. But God loved us, and He gave His Son to die on the cross for us. He gave Jesus to us to be our Savior.

Now if I give you a gift, do you have to pay me for it? No. If I give you something, do you have to work and work for it? No. But there is one thing you must do in order for a gift to be yours. You must RECEIVE IT. That is, you must take it.

Let me show you what I mean:

Here is a little Bible with many wonderful verses in it.
*(I use a small, red Salvation Bible\*)*
Would you like to have this?
*(Several hands will go up)*
Would you like to have this?
*(Speaking in particular to someone near the front)*
Good! Come right up here and take it.

There...now it belongs to her. She didn't have to pay me for that. She didn't have to work and work for it. All she had to do was take it and now it belongs to her.

But suppose she had said, "No, I don't want it." Would it be hers? No, it would not!

God has given the Lord Jesus to you to be your Savior, but if you do not take Him as your Savior, will He be your Savior? No, He will not. If you want Him to be your Savior, you must ask Him to come into your heart. You cannot take Jesus in your hands like a book, but you can take Him into your heart. When you ask Him to come into your heart, and you really mean it, He comes in! He becomes your Savior!

\*Available from: The Little Bible ministry,
Sanatoga, PA 19464

In helping children to come to Christ, keep in mind these essentials:

1. Each child must see that *he has sinned* and be sorry enough for his sins to want to turn from them.
2. He must believe that Jesus died for *his* sins.
3. He must receive the Lord Jesus as *his* Savior.

So often when we talk about what a person has to do to be saved, the discussion seems to be concerned with the *least* one must do. Such "minimum salvation" may take a person to Heaven, but it certainly does not produce a joyful, fruitful Christian. How much better it is to make it our objective to bring children into "maximum salvation" —a full and joyful surrender of their lives to Christ from the beginning. He is worthy—worthy of all that we are and all that we have.

# Part Two

## HOW TO DO IT

### "Get your tools ready and God will use you."

Paul La Botz

There was an awful train wreck. Many were hurt and bleeding. Some were dead. Cries of pain and anguish were heard everywhere. Then someone said, "Is there a doctor here?"

There was a doctor on hand, but, as he saw the broken, bleeding bodies, he cried out helplessly, "Oh, if only I had my tools! If only I had my tools!"

If a skilled doctor needs tools to work effectively, how much more do we need "tools" to deal with eternal souls. Are we concerned enough to prepare ourselves to be effective in winning children to Christ?

# 7

# The Word...
# How to Teach It

**Jesus Christ is not only our
Savior and Lord, but He
is also our Example as the
perfect Teacher.**

Nicodemus said, "We know that Thou art a
teacher come from God." Not only does the Lord
Jesus know all truth, but He Himself *is* the Truth.
Not only does He know the human mind, but He
created it! It is no wonder that men said of Him,
"Never man spake like this man."

What was Jesus' method of teaching? It was
threefold:

> 1) State the truth
> 2) Illustrate the truth
> 3) Apply the truth

For our study of the Master Teacher's method,
let us consider His admonition against anxious
care as presented in Matthew 6:25-34. Here the
Lord Jesus presents one of His greatest and most
beautiful messages.

First, He *stated* the great truth that God's children should not be anxious about what they are
to eat, what they are to drink, or what they are
to wear.

Next, He *illustrated* His message with three wonderfully simple illustrations—the fowls of the air, a man's height, and the flowers of the field.

Then, He *applied* the truth to the consciences of His listeners.

Let us consider the marvelous teaching method of our Lord.

## STATE THE TRUTH...

According to the method used by the Lord Jesus, we should first state the truth as simply as possible. Take a familiar text such as John 3:16 and consider the truths it contains:

> God is *love*
> God *so* loved the world that He *gave*
> God's Gift to us is His *Son*
> God gave Jesus to us to be our *Savior*
> God gave us a Savior because we *needed* a Savior
> *Anyone* can believe in Him and be saved
> If we do not believe in Him, we will *perish*
> Whoever believes in Him *has* everlasting life

## ILLUSTRATE THE TRUTH...

After the Lord stated a truth, He then illustrated it to make it clearer to His listeners. The word "illustrate" comes from the word "in" and the Latin word "lustro" which means "to shine." This tells us what an illustration does—it causes the light to shine in. You use a familiar truth to cause the light to shine in on an unfamiliar truth. Illustrations used in children's messages should be simple and understandable, and they should be about things to which children can relate.

There is another "special" teaching method that will fit some situations—*dramatize the truth*. Many times in the Old Testament, God had His prophets act out a prophecy to vividly impress it on the minds of the people.

When Jesus taught about repentance, He did not give a cold, theological definition. Instead, He told two stories—one of the Prodigal Son and the other of the father with two sons as recorded in Matthew 21:28-32.

Some time ago, I was visiting in the home of a dear missionary brother. This brother recognized that repentance needed to be more strongly emphasized in my messages to children. He proceeded to give me a mini-sermon on the story of the father and the two sons. The hour was late and I was sleepy, but he caught my attention and held it because he dramatized the story.

My friend told of the father's disappointment in the son who said, "I will go, sir," but did not go. Then he told of the hurt which the second son caused to his father's heart when he said, "I won't go!" As he told of the hurt to the father's heart, he dramatized it by bowing his head, placing his right hand over his heart, and walking slowly away.

That night, the aspect of sin as a hurt to God's heart was impressed on me as never before. To this day that scene is vivid in my mind. Why? Because the truth was dramatized.

## APPLY THE TRUTH...

The purpose of teaching God's Word is to produce a decision in the heart, not just to fill the mind with facts. A salesman may have a wonderful presentation, but if he doesn't actually make the sale, he has failed.

If we want children to be saved, we must "draw in the net." We should never pressure children, but we must lovingly and tenderly press home the truth that they must receive Christ or be eternally lost. Often, all that is necessary is the loving invitation, "Wouldn't you like to take the Lord Jesus as your Savior right now so that you can know that you are saved?"

## Suggestions for effective teaching:

● **Arrive early for meetings.** This puts you in control of things from the beginning. For large meetings, you should be there 30 minutes ahead of time. This will give you a chance to look over the situation and to arrange things as you want them.

● **Place the smaller children up front.** If adults are in the audience, ask them to move back so all the children can be up front. It is best not to have too much space between you and the children. Speak simply enough so that the smallest children will understand what you are saying.

● **Tell the children what they can and cannot do.** At the beginning of your message, lay down the ground rules: e.g., "No one talks when I am talking."

● **Make use of the short response.** Let the children answer some questions out loud. The way to have a smart class is to give them the answer before you ask the question. For example: "What is faith? Faith is believing God. Let's say it, class—FAITH IS BELIEVING GOD. What is faith? FAITH IS _____ _____. Good! Say it again —FAITH IS BELIEVING GOD."

● **Have "breaks" in your program.** The attention span of children is rather short for straight lecturing. Use frequent "breaks" —a song or story—to hold the attention. The attention span can be doubled or tripled by using visual aids.

● **Use as many "learning gates" as possible.** We learn by seeing, by hearing, by speaking, and by doing. Make use of the "ear gate," the "eye gate," the "mouth gate," and the "action gate."

● **Know your subject.** The best "teaching tool" of all is a teacher who knows and loves his subject. Modern technology has given us many valuable tools for communicating and teaching, but there never has been, nor ever will be, a substitute for a man or woman of God teaching the Word of God in the power of God's Holy Spirit.

Note: The author is indebted to the writings of James C. McConkey for this outline on how to teach the Word.

# 8

## START with ENTHUSIASM!

... the first few minutes are crucial !

**Most children love to sing, and group singing is one of the best ways to begin a children's meeting.**

**All children can take part and become involved right from the beginning.**

Music is also a wonderful way to teach Bible truth to children. Songs which contain Scripture are especially valuable. My favorite for small children is the chorus to the song, "Believe on the Lord Jesus Christ." (See page 164.)

Another excellent song is John 3:16 sung to the tune of "Silent Night." (Omit the first word "For.") It goes like this:

> John three sixteen, John three sixteen,
> God so loved the world that He
> Gave His only begotten Son,
> that whosoever believeth in Him
> Should not perish but have
> everlasting life.

When it comes time to speak, the first few minutes are crucial. There are several things you can do to get off to a good start. Use one or two of the following:

## CLAPPING GAME

Most children have been bored many times by services not geared to them. When you stand up to talk, they may be thinking, "Oh, no! Not another dull sermon."

One way to get them on your side is to start your program with a game. Children love to play games, and a fun game helps to prepare their hearts for your message. Here is a game that children really enjoy. I tell the children:

> Before I start my program, we're going to play a little game. I know that you like to play games! Here is the way this game goes. I want you to put your hands in front of you like this.

> *Demonstrate by holding your hands in front of you about 8 inches apart, as if you are going to clap.*

> Now I'm going to move my hands like this.

> *Turn sideways slightly and hold your left hand up high and your right hand low. You then let the left hand come down and the right hand go up so that your hands pass vertically.*

Now when my hands pass like this, you clap your hands ONCE, like this.

AS MY HANDS PASS

CHILDREN CLAP *ONCE*

*Demonstrate by holding your hands out in front clapping, and then bringing them back to the position of 8 inches apart.*

Remember, the very second my hands pass, you clap, If everybody does it together, it will sound like one big clap. So STAY TOGETHER! Now, there is one other thing: If you clap when my hands DON'T pass, then you are a rotten egg! So be careful and watch me closely. Now let's try it.

*Go through the procedure several times until the children are clapping properly each time your hands pass and getting their hands back into position for the next pass.*

You are doing real well. Now let's see if you can do it perfectly this time. GET SET...

*This time, start bringing your hands toward a pass quickly, but STOP just short of a pass. Most children will clap.*

IF I STOP MY HANDS WITHOUT PASSING | CHILDREN DON'T CLAP | But those that clap, are "ROTTEN EGGS"

*You will have a lot of "rotten eggs," and you can enjoy laughing with them. There are many variations of this game. Conclude this by starting out slowly and gradually increasing the tempo until the children are clapping enthusiastically. Children enjoy this!*

**CAUTION:** Humor at the beginning of your program is good. It lets the children know that you are a real person and that you enjoy laughing with them. But don't overdo the humor aspect. When you get to the serious part of your message, be serious.

## "The Story Your Hand Wants to Tell You." [2]

This is another good opener, and it states the gospel clearly. I tell it like this:

I want to teach you a story your hand will tell you.

*Hold your left hand toward the children with fingers extended. Use index finger of your right hand to point to the fingers of your left hand.*

Hold your hand out like this. We're going to start with the thumb and go to the little finger. Repeat after me:

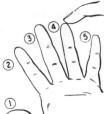

1. I have sinned.
2. God loves me.
3. Jesus died for me.
4. I receive Him.
5. I have everlasting life.

Let's go over it again.
*Repeat the above.*
Now, let me tell you the story.

*Close all fingers of the left hand except the index finger which is pointing up.*

This finger points to God, but look at this thumb!

*Extend thumb out and downward.*

It's going in the other direction. This reminds me that I have sinned. I have done wrong things and said wrong things. I have sinned.

But this finger points to God, and this reminds me that God loves me.

These three fingers remind me of three crosses that stood on a hill outside of Jerusalem. On two of these crosses hung two thieves. But who hung on the middle cross? (Children: "Jesus!") That's right. And this finger reminds me that Jesus died for me.

One of the thieves believed on Jesus, and he asked the Lord Jesus to be his Savior. He took Jesus as his Savior and he was saved. This finger reminds me that I have received Jesus as my Savior.

*Point to fourth finger.*

When you take Jesus as your Savior, *Point to little finger.* you can say, "I have everlasting life." Now you know the story. Let's go over it again.

*Go over this several times until the children know what each finger represents.*

## BIBLE QUIZ

A short Bible quiz makes a good opener, especially for older children. A contest between the boys and the girls makes it especially exciting. You may want to award small prizes to the winning team. I usually use three contestants on each side, but you can use more. I suggest a total of 12 questions—six for each side. Give 20 points for each correct answer.

When a contestant misses a question, let the audience give the correct answer; then go on to the next question for the other team.

If the children have little or no Bible background, you must use very simple questions, such as:

> What was the name of the first man?
>
> Who built a large ship?
>
> Who was the strongest man in the Bible?
>
> Who killed the giant?
>
> What was the name of the first woman?
>
> Who was put in the lion's den?
>
> Who was the wisest man in the Bible?
>
> To whom did God give the Ten Commandments?

For the last four questions, ask the contestants to give you one of the Ten Commandments. This is good preparation for your message.

## SOME DO'S...

**BE ENTHUSIASTIC** in giving the gospel to children. Inwardly, you should be thinking, "I'm glad I'm here. I'm glad you children are here. I have something wonderful to tell you—something that can change your lives. And, Lord, I'm counting on You to help me get it across."

**INVOLVE THE CHILDREN.** Let them participate in your message. How can you do this? By letting them supply certain words as you talk. Be sure the word or words you want them to supply are words they are likely to know. It works better if they are words at the end of a sentence or phrase. For example: "God so loved the _____ that He gave His only begotten _____ that whosoever believeth in Him should not _____ but have _____ _____ ."

**KEEP YOUR COMPOSURE.** Overlook minor distractions. If you lose your inward peace, you are at the mercy of the devil.

**SPEAK LOUDLY ENOUGH.** Children must hear what you are saying. Speak loudly enough so those farthest away can hear you. For large groups, use a PA system.

**LOVE CHILDREN.** The impression you give to children is important. When they sense that you love them, they will respond wonderfully.

**STOP WHEN YOU ARE FINISHED.** The three elements of a good speech are: Stand up, speak up, and shut up!

## AND SOME DON'TS...

**DON'T TALK DOWN TO CHILDREN.**
Children are intelligent. Use words that they understand, but treat them as equals. Sometimes they are smarter than we are!

**DON'T BE AFRAID OF MAKING A MISTAKE.**
Some people are afraid to try to win a child to

Christ for fear of making a mistake. It is better to make a hundred mistakes and lead a child to Christ than to be so afraid of making a mistake that you win no one.

**DON'T BORE CHILDREN.** Learn how to keep their attention. One way of regaining lagging attention is to tell a story or use an illustration.

**DON'T THREATEN CHILDREN** with unreasonable discipline or discipline which you cannot enforce. Win them with love and patience.

> Be your own critic. Constantly evaluate what you are doing. When you find something that works, stick to it!

**"Better a thousand times effective peculiarity than ineffective ordinariness."**
*D.M. Thornton*

# 9

# The All-Time Winner...

## The Wordless Book

Many people associate visual aids with children's work because so many children's workers use them. There is a good reason for using visual aids. We remember only about 10% of what we *hear*, whereas we remember about 50% of what we *see*, and *70% of what we see and hear.*

When it comes to visual aids, the Wordless Book is, in my opinion, the all-time winner. Only the Lord Himself knows how many thousands of children have been won to Christ through the story of the Wordless Book.

What is the Wordless Book? It is, as the name implies, a book with no words. It has only colored pages. Each page represents something in the message of salvation.

>  Gold Page — Heaven
>  Dark Page — sin
>  Red Page — the blood of Christ
>  White Page — the clean heart
>  Green Page — Christian growth

Wordless books come in various sizes, from small pocket sizes to large felt books for use with a flannelboard. If you are using a flannelboard, you will want a copy of the *Wordless Book Visualized.*[3] This contains flannelgraph figures along with instructions for telling the story.

The story of the Wordless Book can be given in five messages — one for each page — or it can be condensed into one salvation message. This is the message I use in children's meetings, and I think it is tops for winning children.

Before making an actual presentation using the flannelgraph figures, study carefully the lessons given in the book and practice placing the figures on the flannelboard. In addition to the instructions in the lesson, I have some suggestions from my experience that may be helpful to you. Begin like this:

>  Have you ever seen a Wordless Book? I call this a Wordless Book because it doesn't have any words! But these pages tell us a wonderful story. This Dark Page stands for sin. That is what we do wrong. The Red Page stands for the Blood of Christ. That means His death for us. He died on the cross for our sins. This White Page stands for the clean heart which we get when we

take Him as our Savior. And this beautiful Gold Page stands for a place where no one will ever be sick, where no one will ever die, where every house is a beautiful mansion, and where the streets are paved with gold. Where is that? Heaven!

## • GOLD PAGE—Heaven

The thrust of this page is: *God loves us and wants us to be in Heaven with Him.*

Begin this page with the account of the ascension. Explain that Jesus is in Heaven now, but that, one day, He is coming back. Then, using the figures in the book, tell about the things that *will not* be in Heaven. [*If you are using the Cloth Heart object lesson, Chapter 10, replace the black paper heart with one made of white felt. Use black pen to put spots on it signifying sins.*] When you complete telling about the things that will not be in Heaven, use two long strips of black felt to make an "X" across this side of the board.

Then use the figures to tell about the things that *will be* in Heaven. Place the figure of Jesus on the board last, impressing upon the children that Jesus *wants* them to be in Heaven with Him.

Conclude the Gold Page like this:

I was in town the other day and they had the prettiest things in the store windows. Why did they put all those pretty things in the store windows? Did they want me OUT of the store or IN the store?

Children: "In the store."

Right! Why does God tell us that Heaven is such a beautiful place? Does God want us OUT of Heaven or IN Heaven?

Children: "In Heaven."

Right! God wants us IN HEAVEN. I wonder if some boy or girl can tell me WHY God wants us in Heaven with Him. [*Wait for a child to hold up his hand.*]

Child: "Because He loves us."

Right! And it doesn't matter who you are, or what you look like, or where you live, God loves YOU and He wants YOU to be in Heaven with Him.

Every one of us can say, "God loves ME!" Let's say it—GOD LOVES ME! That's good, but I think you can do better. This time I want you to point to yourself and say it—GOD LOVES ME! That's better. Now *this* time, I want you to point to yourself and put a good smile on your face and say it like you really mean it—GOD LOVES ME! The most wonderful thing in all the world is to know that God loves you.

---

TAKE TIME TO HAMMER THIS HOME to the children that God loves them and wants them in Heaven with Him.

Children need the assurance that God loves them before you talk to them about their sins.

---

## • DARK PAGE—Sin

The thrust of this page is: *We have sinned, and sin hurts God's heart.*

NOTE: Do not refer to this page as "the Black Page." To do this could imply that the color black is associated with sin. Actually, the Scriptures refer to sins as being "scarlet," or "red," and not black. But it is necessary to use the Red Page for the Blood of Christ; therefore, we must use the Dark Page for sin. You can explain to the children that, in the Bible, darkness is a type of sin.

Begin this page like this:

Suppose you knew that someone loved you more than anything in the world, loved you enough to die for you. Would you want to do anything to hurt them? No, of course not. God loves you more than anything. He loved you enough to die for you. Now I am going to talk to you about something that hurts His heart. What is it? It is SIN! Sin hurts God's heart.

Sin is what we do wrong. Sin hurts us, sin hurts other people, but the worst thing about sin is this—sin hurts God's heart. Let's say it together—*Sin hurts God's heart.*

Let's say it again—SIN HURTS GOD'S HEART.

I want to tell you how sin came into the world. God created the earth and the universe. He created a beautiful garden called "the garden of Eden." Then God created the first man, Adam. He created a wife for Adam, and her name was Eve. [*Proceed with the story of Adam and Eve.*]

After telling how Adam and Eve brought sin into the world, talk about the sins we commit. Remember: Relating the true stories of what *other* children have confessed as sin is one of the best ways of showing children *their* sins. [*The Cloth Heart Object Lesson, Chapter 10, is excellent here.*]

IMPORTANT: Don't rush through this section. Give the Holy Spirit an opportunity to bring conviction of sins. Continue:

The Bible says that we have all sinned. I believe that right now God is speaking to your heart and reminding you of some of the wrong things you have done. The Bible says that the wages of sin is death. This means to be separated from God, forever, in a terrible place which God has prepared for the devil and his followers.

In going from the Dark Page to the Red Page, it is good to use an illustration. The best illustration I have found is "Grandmother's Knitting Needle." [*See Chapter 10.*]

## • RED PAGE—The Blood of Christ

The thrust of this page is: *Jesus took our punishment and died for our sins.* Continue narration:

> The Bible says, "The wages of sin is death." This means that something had to die for sin. Before Jesus came, God told the people to bring a lamb and offer it as a sacrifice for their sins. That little lamb died for that person's sins. Now we know why Jesus is called "the Lamb of God." He died for our sins.

Go directly into the account of the crucifixion. This is a most holy and solemn message and should be given in a serious manner. It must touch you deeply if it is to touch the children deeply. In concluding this page, point out that one thief repented and trusted Christ as his Savior, and he was saved. The other thief did not repent or trust Christ and he was lost. If we repent and believe in Jesus, we will be saved. If we do not, we will be lost forever.

NOTE: From my experience, I have found that it is best to give the children an opportunity to receive Christ into their hearts at the conclusion of the Red Page rather than at the conclusion of the message. It is not necessary for the children to come forward. They can be saved right in their places. (See Chapter 11 for information on how to give the invitation.)

## • WHITE PAGE—The Clean Heart

The thrust of this page is: *Jesus forgives us of every sin when He comes into our heart.*

Following the invitation, you move to the White Page and the story of the resurrection. The resurrection of Christ is the foundation of the Christian faith. There should be a note of joy and triumph in your voice and manner as you give the account of the resurrection. Impress on the children that the Lord Jesus is the *risen* Savior and that He has *all* power in Heaven and in earth.

NOTE: If you are giving the story of the Wordless Book in one message, conclude with this page; otherwise the message will be too long.

## • GREEN PAGE—Christian Growth

The thrust of this page is: *We must grow in the Christian life.* Follow the story as given in the instruction book.

Suggestions For Using Flannelboard.

- When using a flannelboard, place a small, portable, 150 watt spotlight in front of your board so that the light shines directly on it. This will give "life" to your scenes. (It is not necessary or desirable to darken the room.)

- Keep flannelboard scenes simple and uncluttered. You do not have to use all the figures provided. Leave off unnecessary figures so as to center attention on the main subject.

- Keep the figures for each scene in a separate file folder. If you are using this story frequently you may want to purchase an additional set of figures so that you have a set of figures for *each* scene rather than having to use the same figure for several scenes.

NOTE: The Wordless Book is also available in a flash-card edition. This is inexpensive and easy to use. For further information write: The Mailbox Club, 404 Eager Road, Valdosta, Ga. 31602

# 10

# Getting it Across...

## with illustrations and object lessons

In winning children to Christ, illustrations and object lessons are invaluable. There are many excellent illustrations which help children to understand salvation.

## • ILLUSTRATION

The most effective illustration I have ever used is "Grandmother's Knitting Needle."[4] Here is the way I tell it:

> I once heard a story that made a great impression on me. The man in this story was raised by his grandmother. He said, "My grandmother was a fine Christian lady and she loved me. But when I was a boy, I had a bad habit. I took things that did not belong to me. My grandmother whipped me and whipped me about stealing, but that didn't stop me. When I saw something I wanted, I just took it.
>
> "One day my grandmother called me over and said, 'Son, I have been whipping you

and whipping you about this stealing and it hasn't seemed to do much good. I love you too much to let you continue doing this. The next time you come home with something that doesn't belong to you, I'm going to take one of these knitting needles and heat it red hot in the fire. Then I am going to burn your thieving hand with it.' "

He said, "That really scared me, and I didn't take anything for a long time. Then, one day, I went back to my old ways. When I came home, I had some things that I had stolen. I was trying to hide them when my grandmother saw me.

"She felt so bad because she knew that I was stealing again. She said, 'Where did you get those things?' I couldn't answer. Then she said, 'Son, you know what I told you and you know that I always do what I say I am going to do.'

"She went over and put the knitting needle in the fire. When it was red hot, she called me over by the fire. She got something and picked up the needle and said, 'Son, hold out your hand.' I was trembling as I held out my hand.

"Then my grandmother paused and said, 'Son, you deserve this, but I am going to take your punishment for you.' With that, she dropped my hand and pierced her own hand with the red hot needle.

"Then she held out her bleeding hand and

said, 'Son, don't take your eyes from it. This is what your sin cost me.'

"That day I understood the seriousness of my sins when I saw what it cost one whom I loved. Never since have I touched anything that did not belong to me."

Notice that this story contains the essentials of the gospel. The boy had sinned, therefore he deserved to be punished. The grandmother loved the boy and did not want to punish him, but she had to keep her word. The grandmother solved the problem by taking his punishment and bearing it herself. This brought true repentance to the boy's heart. Conclude with the following:

The grandmother took that boy's punishment. Why did she do it? Because she...

Children: "Loved him."

Right! And the Lord Jesus took our punishment. Why did He do it? Because He...

Children: "Loved us!"

## • OBJECT LESSON NO. 1— Cloth Heart

Purpose: To illustrate how the blood of Christ takes away our sins.

Materials needed:

1. Iodine solution. Purchase a small bottle of iodine tincture at a drug store.

2. Hypo solution. Purchase 4¼ oz. bag of Hypo clearing agent (Kodak Cat. 153 3942) at a camera shop. This can be re-used many times.

3. Cloth hearts. Make out of white cotton cloth. These can be washed out and re-used.

The iodine solution represents sin. Put solution in larger bottle with small opening and a tight-fitting cap. Label this bottle SIN.

The Hypo solution represents the blood of Christ. Use a large mouth jar, such as a peanut butter jar, and cover it with red plastic tape. Pour one-half of the Hypo crystals into jar and mix with 6 oz. of water.

The hearts can be made out of plain, white cotton cloth, such as an old sheet. Hearts should be about 8″ in width and height.

PROCEDURE: Show the clean heart. Explain that Adam and Eve were created with clean hearts, but Adam and Eve disobeyed God. Using SIN bottle put an iodine spot in the center of the heart. Tell the children that this is an iodine solution but that it represents sin. Tell how Adam and Eve passed their sinful natures on to their children and the whole world—Cain killed his own brother.

Now take up the matter of our sins. Talk about specific sins, such as lying, stealing, disobeying parents, disobeying teachers, talking back to parents, cheating, hating people, bad talk, etc. Fold the heart in half and apply an iodine spot for each sin. This will make two spots on the heart when it is unfolded. When you finish, you will have many spots on the heart.

Explain that we cannot go to Heaven with sin in our hearts, but God loved us and sent His Son to die for us. Tell how He forgives us of every sin when we take Christ as our Savior. While you are talking, put the heart with the spots into the red jar. It will take only a moment for the Hypo solution to remove the spots. Remove heart from jar, squeezing out excess solution. Unfold to show that the spots are gone. Isaiah 1:18 is good to quote here—"Though your sins be as scarlet, they shall be as white as snow."

IMPORTANT: *Practice this before an actual presentation!*

**USE PROPER PRECAUTIONS WITH THE CHEMICALS. KEEP THEM AWAY FROM THE CHILDREN. KEEP BOTTLE TIGHTLY CAPPED WHEN NOT IN USE. STORE UPRIGHT.**

## • OBJECT LESSON NO. 2 —

Purpose: To teach children that we were made to be indwelled by God.

Items needed: Empty Coke bottle and light bulb.

Here is the way I tell this:

Boys and girls, I have learned a most wonderful thing from my study of the Bible! You say, "What is it that you have learned?" I have learned WHY God made us. He made us to *contain* something. Let me show you what I mean. [*Hold up empty Coke bottle.*] Here is something that was made to contain a certain thing. What was this made to contain?

Children: "Coke!"

Right! This was made to contain Coke. Now here is something that was made to contain something else. [*Hold up light bulb.*] What was this made to contain?

Children: "Light!" (They may say "Electricity.")

Right! The bottle was made to contain Coke, and the light bulb was made to contain light or electricity.

Now, you and I were made to contain something—I should say SOME-ONE—the most wonderful person in all the universe. I wonder if you can tell me who that is?

Children: "God!"

That's right! We were made to contain God! And it's the most wonderful thing in all the world when God comes to live in your heart! Jesus is God, and when we ask Him to come into our heart, He comes in. He said, "If anyone—any boy or any girl—will hear My voice and ask Me to come in, I WILL COME IN."

---

"At every step in leading a child to Christ, pray for, look for, and expect the Holy Spirit to convict of sin, to reveal the truth of the Gospel, and to illumine the child's mind so he can grasp saving truth."

*—Irvin Overholtzer*

# 11

# Drawing in the Net...

## How to Give the Invitation

**We now come to the most important part of the message — inviting the child to receive Christ as his Savior. Unless Christ is received, the child will not be "born again."**

Remember, these three things must take place at conversion:

1. The child must see that *he has sinned,* and be sorry enough for his sins to want to stop doing them.

2. He must *believe* that Jesus died for his sins.

3. He must *receive* the Lord Jesus as his Savior.

Giving the invitation is "drawing in the net." This is a most serious time. We must be totally dependent on the Holy Spirit. You and I cannot give spiritual life to anyone. Only the Holy Spirit can do this. He works best when we are very calm inside, trusting Him to do His work in the hearts of the children.

With these things in mind, let us see how we lead up to the invitation and how to give it. If you are using the Wordless Book, you can conclude the Red Page like this:

One of the thieves believed on the Lord Jesus and he asked Jesus to save him. He said, "Lord, remember me when You come into Your kingdom." Jesus turned to that dying man and said, "Today shalt thou be with Me in paradise." That man received Jesus as his Savior and he was saved. The other thief did not take Jesus as his Savior, and he was lost forever.

Sometimes, when a boy or girl starts to ask the Lord Jesus to come into his or her heart, the old devil will say, "It's all right to do that *some* day, but not now." He likes to tell us to wait and wait because he wants us to be lost. But when does God tell us to be saved? Right

_____ .

Children: "Now!"

Do you know why God tells us to be saved now? Because we don't know how long we are going to live. [ *Tell a true story showing how suddenly and unexpectedly death can come. Don't make this too sad. The object is not to play on the children's emotions but to show them that life is uncertain; therefore, they should make a decision NOW.* ]

Jesus said that our heart is like a house. He said, "Behold, I stand at the door and knock. If any man, or any boy or girl, hears My voice and opens the door, I WILL COME IN."

If I came to see you, I would not walk right into your house. That would not be polite. I would knock at the door. If you saw me outside and you wanted me to come in, what would you say?

Children: "Come in."

That's right, and when you ask the Lord Jesus to come into your heart, He comes in. [ *If you are using the Cloth Heart object lesson, put the heart with the iodine spots into the red jar with the Hypo solution.* ] When Jesus comes into your heart, He forgives you of *every* sin. [ *Remove cloth heart from jar, squeezing out excess solution. Unfold to show that the spots are gone.* ]

Now I want us to bow our heads in prayer. No one looking around. I am going to ask a few questions. I want you to keep your heads bowed and your eyes closed but speak right out if you know the answers. [ *This is the actual invitation and consists of six questions and the prayer.* ]

1. Do you believe that Jesus Christ is the Son of God?

    Children: "Yes."

2. Do you believe that the Lord Jesus died on the cross for *your* sins?

Children: "Yes."

3. Does Jesus love you?

   Children: "Yes."

4. Is the Lord Jesus willing to be *your* Savior?

   Children: "Yes."

5. Do you think the Lord Jesus would come into your heart right now if you would ask Him to?

   Children: "Yes."

6. When do you think you should ask the Lord Jesus to come into *your* heart?

   Children: "Now!"

Keep your heads bowed and your eyes closed... no one looking around. If you know that you have sinned and you truly want Jesus to come into your heart to be your Savior, just slip up your hand.

Yes, I see your hand...yes, I see your hand... No one looking around. Now if you really mean it, I want you to pray in your heart after me:

> Lord Jesus, I know that I have sinned, and I am truly sorry for my sins. I know that my sins have hurt Your heart, and I do want to stop doing them. I thank You for loving me so much and for dying for me. Please come into my heart and be my Savior. I take you as my Savior right now. Come in today. Come in to stay. Come into my heart, Lord Jesus.

Conclude this part of the invitation with prayer, then continue with the message.

Did you really mean it when you asked the Lord Jesus to come into your heart?

Children: "Yes."

What did Jesus say that He would do? He said, "I will _____ _____."

Children: "Come in!"

Did you ask Him to come into *your* heart?

Children: "Yes."

Does Jesus keep His Word?

Children: "Yes."

Then where is Jesus now? Is He out of your heart or IN your heart?

Children: "In my heart!"

That's right, and once the Lord Jesus comes to live in your heart, He will never leave you. He said, "I will never leave you." Let's say it together: "I WILL NEVER LEAVE YOU!"

In meetings where I do not have the opportunity to ask the children to come forward, I give the invitation as I have done here. Many children are saved right in their places. However, where possible, it is best to counsel with those who have indicated that they want to be saved. If you have the opportunity to counsel with the children, you can say:

Let's bow our heads in prayer. If you have asked the Lord Jesus to come into your heart, I want you to thank Him right now for coming into your heart. [*After a short prayer of thanks, continue.*] While our heads are bowed and our eyes closed, I want all of you who raised your hands to go quietly with _____ into the other room. We want to talk to you a few minutes and show you some verses from God's Word. If you did not raise your hand but you really want to ask Jesus into your heart, you may go also. The rest of you remain in your places.

After all have left, offer a short prayer for those who are being counseled and then continue with your message or with some singing. It is important to keep the remaining children occupied while the others are being counseled.

---

**CAUTION**: In giving an invitation we must be careful not to push children. It is in the very nature of a child to respond and to want to please adults. This is good because it means that children readily respond to the gospel. But it is not good in that children can easily be led or pushed into decisions they are not ready for. We must trust the Holy Spirit to do His work, and we must respect His timing. Decisions are meaningful and have spiritual value only when they are the result of the Holy Spirit's working in hearts.

# 12

# Effective Counseling

## How to Lead a Child to Christ

An invitation should be included in your message even if you cannot ask the children to come forward. Many children are saved right in their places while the invitation is being given. But, when possible, you should counsel personally with the children about their salvation.

The first and most basic principle in counseling is: USE THE WORD OF GOD.

We are born again by faith in God's Word. The Bible says, "Being born again, not of corruptible seed, but of incorruptible, *by the word of God...*"

# Suggestions For Effective Counseling:

● **Find out the child's spiritual condition** and why he came for counseling. He might just want you to pray for his sick dog!

● **Have the child read the Scriptures out loud.** Be sure to have a readable copy of the Bible to use. A large print copy of the New Testament is excellent for use in counseling children. A Horton's *Gospel of John* (Moody Press) is also very good for counseling older children, and you can let them keep it.

● **Answer objections from the Word of God.** Generally, children do not have many excuses or objections. But if some question is bothering the child, use the Word of God to answer it.

● **Don't use too many verses.** It is better to use a few verses and make sure the child understands them than to confuse him with many verses.

● **Go over a verse until the child understands it.** Much of counseling is simply going over a verse again and again until the child grasps the meaning. Difficult and archaic words must be thoroughly explained.

● **Depend on the Holy Spirit to give illumination.** It is one thing to understand a verse mentally; it is another thing to "see" the truth by the Spirit's enabling. We are utterly dependent upon the Holy Spirit to reveal spiritual truth to the child.

● **Bring the child to rest his faith on God's Word.** We are not saved by some feeling or experience; we are saved by faith in God's Word. Answer any questions that come up, but do not get sidetracked. Constantly direct the child's attention to what God says in His Word.

Now, let us go through an actual counseling session in leading a child to Christ. (It is always good to use the child's name in counseling.)

Counselor: Jimmy, I'm glad you came to talk with me. I want to ask you a question. If you were to die tonight—some people die very suddenly, you know—do you know for sure that you would go to Heaven?

Jimmy: No, I don't.

Counselor: I wonder if you know the *way* to be saved. Some people think that the way to be saved is by being good or being baptized or joining the church. But the Bible doesn't say that. The Bible says that all of us are sinners. We have all broken God's laws. We have all sinned. I want to show you a verse from God's Word. It's Romans 3:23. Here, read it.

Jimmy: "For all have sinned, and come short of the glory of God."

Counselor: God says here that we have all sinned. Has God spoken to you about some of the wrong things that you have said and done? Do you know that you have sinned?

Jimmy: Yes.

Counselor: I have sinned too, Jimmy. The Bible says that the punishment for sin is to be separated from God forever in a terrible place which the Bible calls hell. But God loves us and He does not want us to go to that place. Now, let's turn to John 3:16. You may already know this verse, but I want you to read it to me.

Jimmy: "For God so loved the world that He gave His only begotten Son, that whosoever believeth in Him should not perish, but have everlasting life."

Counselor: Very good, Jimmy. Whom does God mean when He says "the world"?

Jimmy: I guess He means all of us.

Counselor: That's right. We're in the world, aren't we? And God loves us! In fact, He loves us so much that He gave something very precious to us. What did God give to us? Read the verse and tell me.

Jimmy: "For God so loved the world that He

gave His only begotten Son"...He gave His *Son* to us.

Counselor: Right! And that means that He gave His Son, the Lord Jesus, to die on the cross for our sins. He gave Jesus to us to be our Savior. If I give you something, do you have to pay me for it?

Jimmy: No.

Counselor: If I give you something, do you have to work and work for it?

Jimmy: No.

Counselor: But there is one thing you *must do* in order for a gift to be yours. You must RECEIVE IT. That is, you must take it. When you take a gift, then it is yours. God has given the Lord Jesus to you to be your Savior, but you must take Him into your heart as your very own Savior.

Counselor: Now let us turn to John chapter 1, verse 12. Verse 11 says that Jesus came to His own people, the Jews, and they did not receive Him. They did not believe on Him. Now read verse 12 to me.

Jimmy: "But as many as received Him, to them gave He power to become the sons of God, even to them that believe on His name."

Counselor: This verse tells us that we become a child of God by *receiving* Jesus into our heart as our Savior. Jimmy, do you believe that Jesus is the Son of God?

Jimmy: Yes.

Counselor: Do you believe that He died on the cross for your sins?

Jimmy: Yes.

Counselor: Does Jesus love you?

Jimmy: Yes.

Counselor: Do you believe that He would come into your heart right now and be your Savior if you would ask Him to?

Jimmy: Yes, I do.

Counselor: Would you like to take the Lord Jesus as *your* Savior right now?

Jimmy: I sure would.

Counselor: Good! Let's bow our heads and you talk to the Lord Jesus in your own words. Tell Him that you know that you have sinned and that you are sorry for your sins. Thank Him for dying on the cross for your sins and ask Him to come into your heart.

Jimmy: Lord Jesus, I know that I have sinned,

and I'm sorry for my sins. I thank You for dying on the cross for me. I want You to come into my heart and forgive me of my sins. Please come into my heart right now and be my Savior.

Counselor: Very good, Jimmy. Now, I want you to look at John 3:36. Read it out loud.

Jimmy: "He that believeth on the Son hath everlasting life: and he that believeth not the Son shall not see life; but the wrath of God abideth on him."

Counselor: That's fine, Jimmy. Notice that this verse is talking about two groups of people in the world. Everybody is in one group or the other, and it says something about each group. See if you can tell me the two groups.

Jimmy: The good people and the sinners.

Counselor: No, we are all sinners. Look at the verse again and see what it says.

Jimmy: I see now...it's the ones that believe on the Son and the ones that don't believe.

Counselor: Right! And everybody is in one group or the other. We believe on Jesus, or we don't believe on Him. Which group are *you* in?

Jimmy: I'm in the group that believes on Him.

Counselor: Good! What does God say about you if you are in this group?

Jimmy: He says that I will have everlasting life.

Counselor: No, it doesn't say that, Jimmy. Read it again.

Jimmy: "He that believeth on the Son *hath* everlasting life..."

Counselor: That's right, and the word *"hath"* means that you *have* it right now. Take my watch, for example. Would I say "I *will* have it," or "I have it *right now*"?

Jimmy: You have it right now.

Counselor: Right! And what does God say that you have if you believe on the Lord Jesus?

Jimmy: He says that I have everlasting life.

Counselor: Do you have everlasting life?

Jimmy: Yes, I do.

Counselor: How do you know you have it?

Jimmy: Because it says so right here.

Counselor: Good, Jimmy! That's what I want you to do—put your faith in God's Word. Suppose you leave here and somebody tells you that he doesn't believe you

|  | have everlasting life. Would you rather believe him or believe God? |
|---|---|
| Jimmy: | I would rather believe God! |
| Counselor: | Right! Now, let's turn to another verse. This is in John's epistle, and it's near the back of the Bible—1 John 5:13. I'm going to quote this verse, and I want you to check me in the Bible because I'm going to make a mistake. I want you to see if you can catch the mistake. Are you ready? Look at the verse and listen carefully. "These things have I written unto you that believe on the name of the Son of God that ye may THINK that ye have eternal life..." |
| Jimmy: | You said "think," but this says "know." |
| Counselor: | Good, Jimmy. I'm glad you caught the mistake. Now read it correctly. |
| Jimmy: | "These things have I written unto you that believe on the name of the Son of God that ye may KNOW that ye have eternal life, and that ye may believe on the name of the Son of God." |
| Counselor: | Very good, Jimmy. Do you believe on the name of the Son of God—that is, do you believe in Jesus as your Savior? |
| Jimmy: | Yes, I do. |
| Counselor: | Then what does God tell you in this |

verse that He wants you to know?

Jimmy: He wants me to know that I have eternal life.

Counselor: Right! Do you KNOW that you have eternal life?

Jimmy: Yes, I do.

Counselor: How do you know that you have it?

Jimmy: Because it says so right here in the Bible.

Counselor: That's right, Jimmy. We know we are saved because *God says so!*

God Said It
I Believe It
That <u>Settles</u> It!

## Some Points to Remember

● Endeavor to bring the child to the assurance that he is saved NOW. This assurance must be based on the Word of God.

● Explain to the child that, even after we are saved, we still have a sinful nature. We will still be tempted to do wrong things, and at times, we will sin.

● Show the child what to do when he sins. He is

to confess his sins to God at once, according to 1 John 1:9. Assure him that he is still in God's family.

● Warn him that, if he continues to sin willfully, God will chasten—"spank"—him. (See Hebrews 12:6,7.) Explain to him that God loves us and does not like to chasten us, but He loves us too much to let us go on in sin.

● Encourage him to confess Christ to others by asking him to tell at least five of his friends that he has received Christ as his Savior.

● Help get him established in a local, Bible-believing church. He needs the fellowship of other Christian children.

## Remember — Children Are Children!

Don't be surprised if some of the same ones come again and again for counseling. At the close of my camp one summer, a little boy ran excitedly to meet his mother with these words, "Mother, I got saved *three times* this week!"

We may smile at this, but we must remember that we are dealing with children. Often a child does not grasp the truth the first time he hears it, even though he may say he does understand it. We must be patient and go over the verses as many times as necessary to give the child assurance.

Children's workers should also realize that, when a child commits his life to the Lord, he is doing so on the basis of his present understanding. This may need to be ratified when the child is older. When a child comes forward and again commits his life to the Lord, it does not mean that the previous commitment was insincere, but rather that he is making his present commitment in the light of the new understanding he has of his life and of the future.

WORLDTEAM co-founder E.V. Thompson said that, when he was growing up, he went forward many times to commit his life to the Lord. This was not insincerity on his part but rather the evidence of a sensitive spirit and a desire to give his all to God.

## Win the Family!

Any work with children which does not include a ministry to the parents is short-sighted and of limited value. God's plan is that the parents be saved and grow spiritually so they can teach their children and be an example to them.

God saves us as individuals, but His desire and plan is that entire households be saved. The ark which God commanded Noah to prepare was not for him alone but for his whole family. God said to Noah, "Come thou and all thy house into the ark." And the paschal lamb, that wonderful type of Christ, was not for an individual but for a household. These and other examples in the Bible show us how important is the household in the sight of God.

By God's grace may we seek to win households to Christ. If you have a genuine love for a child, you have a unique opportunity to reach the parents.

# 13

# Mailing God's Message

## Bible Correspondence Courses

- **Children like to belong to a club.**
- **They like to receive mail.**
- **They like to learn about God.**

One of the most effective ways of winning children to Christ and grounding them in the Word of God is through Bible correspondence lessons. We discovered this through our own experience.

We were reaching thousands of children with a flannelgraph presentation of the gospel. Many of them were coming to Christ. We needed some type of follow-up to lead them into an assurance of their salvation and to ground them in the Word of God.

In 1965, we began writing Bible lessons to fulfill this need. The Lord gave us a name for our courses that is especially appealing to children — The Mailbox Club. Children like to belong to a club, they like to receive mail, and they like to learn about God.

There was such an enthusiastic response to our first course that we were encouraged to write additional courses on deeper truths so that the children could grow spiritually and become fruitful, victorious Christians.

We *know* that Bible correspondence lessons work! Any believer who loves the Lord can win children to Christ with Bible lessons!

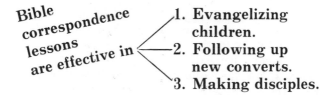

Bible correspondence lessons are effective in

1. Evangelizing children.
2. Following up new converts.
3. Making disciples.

## 1. Evangelizing Children

When we began writing lessons, we were thinking primarily of follow-up for new converts. But we have discovered that the lessons are a wonderful way of *winning* children to the Lord.

I recall stopping at a motel one afternoon. A young boy about 10 years old showed me to my room. I could not detain this boy to talk to him about the Lord, so I handed him a Bible correspondence lesson and said, "Son, here's something I think you will be interested in. Just read it and fill out the answer sheet. Mail it back to me, and

I'll send you another lesson. There are seven lessons. When you complete them, I'll send you a beautiful certificate with your name on it."

A few days later, his answer sheet arrived. At the bottom of the sheet the question was asked, "Have you received the Lord Jesus as your Savior?" He answered, "Yes." In answer to the next question, "When?" he wrote, "Right now!"

I was in the mountains of North Carolina one summer working on a new course for The Mailbox Club. Late each afternoon, to relieve some of the tensions of the work, I went jogging along the back roads.

One afternoon, I saw a small group of children playing by the road. The next afternoon, I had my back pocket stuffed with Mailbox Club lessons. When I saw the children, I stopped and chatted with them, explaining what The Mailbox Club was. Then I handed each of them a Lesson 1. Very shortly, I began hearing from one of these children, a little girl named Sandra.

Six weeks later, I received a letter from a Mrs. Long, the housemother at a boarding school for mountain children. She explained that she had seen Sandra's lessons and liked them. She wondered if I could send lessons for the other 23 girls in her dormitory. We sent them immediately.

Ten days later, the mail brought one of the most thrilling letters I have ever received. Mrs. Long wrote that she had given the lessons to the girls to study for their devotions before going to bed.

"A short time later," wrote Mrs. Long, "I heard a knock at my door. When I opened the door, there stood one of the girls with a Mailbox Club lesson in her hand and tears streaming down her cheeks. 'Mrs. Long,' she said, 'I want to ask Jesus to come into my heart. Will you pray with me?' "

Mrs. Long continued, "I prayed with her and rejoiced with her that she had trusted Christ as her Savior. Before we were through, there was another knock at my door. There stood another girl, lesson in hand, wanting to ask Jesus into her heart. Before I got through counseling her, another girl was at the door. It seemed that little girls were coming to my room all night long! That night eighteen girls received Christ as Savior!"

**"All thy children shall be taught of the Lord; and great shall be the peace of thy children."** Isaiah 54:13

## 2. Following Up New Converts

In the physical realm, God provides parents for each baby. A new-born baby must be fed, loved, and cared for. This is no less true in the spiritual realm. Miss Helen Odenwelder said, "We who bring a spiritual babe into this world have a responsibility to see that he is fed and cared for."

It is foolish and short-sighted to devote all our efforts to getting children to receive Christ and then drop them like a proverbial hot cake. With the proper follow-up, we can help them become fruitful and victorious Christians and thus multiply the effectiveness of our work.

A Chinese girl in New York wrote, "Yes, the Lord Jesus has certainly come to live in my heart! And it's going to be forever and ever! I guess I owe all this to The Mailbox Club, because it was with the help of these lessons which taught me how to receive the Lord as my Savior. It also taught me about eternity, our enemies, what's right and what's wrong...These lessons have been like a Sunday school class to me. I was not able to go to church or Sunday school because my parents are non-Christians..."

> **"We who bring a spiritual babe into this world have a responsibility to see that he is fed and cared for."** Helen Odenwelder

## 3. Making Disciples

It is wonderful when a child is saved and led to an assurance of his salvation, but we have a further responsibility. We must make disciples. After all, this is what our Lord told us to do.

New converts should be taught the great truths of the Bible in a *systematic* way. How can you do this? One way is through Bible correspondence lessons.

The mother of a twenty-year-old son wrote, "You spoke to my son when he was seven years old. Through your talk and the Mailbox Club lessons, you taught him to love the Bible and he has loved it ever since."

A teen-age girl wrote, "I have been on your mailing list for a good number of years. When I first became involved in your studies, I was five years old. I have thoroughly enjoyed the lessons... I would like to know if you still have the lessons for the age group from 6 to 10 years old. I would like to start the children at my church with these lessons. They were inspiring to me and I think they would help the children in my community."

The Mailbox Club has advanced courses to teach deeper truths on the person and work of the Lord Jesus and the truths of our union with Christ in His death, burial, and resurrection. Children, as well as adults, need to know and grasp these wonderful truths.

Padget Wilkes said, "When we lead a soul to Christ, we lead but one. When, however, like Joshua of old, we are able to lead a saint into the land that flows with milk and honey, we are the means of saving a thousand. The soul thus empowered becomes another 'Joshua,' a center of light and blessing and power, and himself a winner of souls."

> **"No other agency can penetrate so deeply, witness so daringly, abide so persistently, and influence so irresistibly as the printed page."** *Dr. Samuel Zwemer*

# 14

## Teaching
## Victorious Living
### TO CHILDREN

"Thanks be to God, which
giveth us the victory through
our Lord Jesus Christ."
1 Corinthians 15:57

It is wonderful to lead children to Christ, but
our work doesn't end there. We need to teach them
the way of victory.

How sad it is to see children and
young people won to the Lord and then
left to struggle in their own strength
against the world, the flesh, and
the devil.

It is not enough to tell young Christians, "Read
your Bible, pray, and go to church." Temptations
are real, the lusts of the flesh are real, the pull
of the world is real, and the power of Satan is real.
Children need to know God's way of victory.

Certain truths are absolutely basic to a life of
victory. Children readily grasp these truths when
they are presented to them in a simple, understandable way. We will try to explain them as
simply as we can, but you will have to put them

in your own words when teaching them to the children.

### TEACH THE CHILD THAT he can KNOW he is saved.

A child must have assurance of his salvation if he is to know victory in his life. Such assurance must be based on the Word of God.

Perhaps the clearest and simplest passage in the Bible regarding assurance is John chapter 10. In this passage Jesus said, "My sheep hear My voice, and I know them, and they follow Me: And I give unto them eternal life."

These words are easily understood by children. When we take Jesus as our Savior, we become one of His "sheep." What does Jesus give His sheep? He gives them "eternal life." How long is that? It is forever and ever.

Jesus says further, "They shall never perish, neither shall any man pluck them out of My hand. My Father, which gave them Me, is greater than

all; and no man is able to pluck them out of My Father's hand." When explaining this to a child, we can emphasize that he is in Christ's hand and in the Father's hand, and no one can ever take him out of their hands.

To be balanced in our teaching, we should explain to the child that Jesus' sheep follow Him. If we are not following Jesus, we cannot claim these promises.

**TEACH THE CHILD THAT** Christ is in him.

The truth, "Christ in you," is one which is readily accepted and understood by children. If the child understands that he was saved by taking Jesus into his heart, it is easy for him to understand and grasp the truth that Christ is now living in him. The Apostle Paul said, "Christ liveth in me." We can say this too if we have taken Him as our Savior.

One aspect of this truth that is especially helpful to children in overcoming temptation is that Christ, who lives in us, is greater and stronger than the devil, who is in the world. The Bible says, "Greater is He that is in you, than he that is in the world." This should be carefully explained to the child and he should be urged to memorize this verse  1 John 4:4 .

### TEACH THE CHILD THAT he is IN CHRIST.

Not only is Christ in us, but we are also "in Christ." When we received Christ as our Savior, God put us IN CHRIST. 1 Corinthians 1:30 says, "Of Him (of God) are you in Christ Jesus..."

This little phrase, "in Christ" or "in Him," occurs many times in the New Testament. God wants us to know that we are IN CHRIST. This truth is the key to understanding God's way of victory.

What does it mean to be IN CHRIST? It means to share in all that Christ is and all that He has done. We shared in His death, His burial, and His resurrection. The Bible says that we were "crucified with Christ," and "buried with Him," and "raised with Him."

How could we be "crucified with Christ"? One of the best ways of teaching this truth to a child is "The Paper Man in a Book" illustration. Cut out a little paper man and proceed as follows:

"Boys and girls, the Bible says that, when we are saved, God puts us IN CHRIST. Let's say that this little paper man represents us and this book represents Christ. God says that He put us IN CHRIST, so let's take the little man and put him in the book.

"The little man is now in the book. Suppose we place the book on the floor. Where is the little man now? He is on the floor because he is in the book.

"Suppose we place the book on the top of a piano. Where is the little man now? He is on top of the piano because he is in the book.

"Suppose we wrap the book and mail it to New York. Where is the little man now? He is in New York because he is in the book.

"Suppose we hold the book under water. What happens to the little man? He is under water also because he is in the book. WHATEVER happens to the book happens to the little man also because he is in the book.

"When God saved us, He put us IN CHRIST on the cross. What happened to Christ happened to us because we were IN CHRIST. When Christ was crucified, we were crucified with Him; when He died, we died with Him, when He was buried, we were buried with Him; when He rose again, we rose again with Him."

## TEACH THE CHILD THAT, IN CHRIST, he has been delivered from Satan's power.

Through our union with Christ in His death and resurrection, we have been delivered from Satan's Kingdom of Darkness and "transplanted" or placed into the Kingdom of God's dear Son.

When we were writing Course III of The Mailbox Club lessons, we used simple language and illustrations to present this truth. Here is a brief summary of the way it is presented in the lessons:

The first man, Adam, was created by God. Because Adam was the first man, he was the head of the human race. What he did affected the whole human race.

Before Adam's fall, sin had already entered the universe. Satan had rebelled against God, and a third of the angels of Heaven had followed him in his rebellion. Satan and his followers make up what is known as "the Kingdom of Darkness."

When Adam sinned by disobeying God, he took sides with Satan and came into the Kingdom of Darkness and under the power of sin. Because he was the head of the human race, Adam brought the whole human family into the Kingdom of Darkness and under the power of sin.

Adam was created sinless, but after he disobeyed God, he had a sinful nature. Adam passed his sinful nature on to his children and to the whole human race. The Bible says, "by one man's disobedience many were made sinners."

The Lord Jesus came into the world to deliver us from the Kingdom of Darkness and from the power of sin. Jesus Himself was never under the power of sin, but on the cross He took our place in the Kingdom of Darkness. Our sins were laid on Him.

What happened when Christ died? He passed out of the Kingdom of Darkness where sin reigns. He was buried, and He rose again the third day. He rose in a new Kingdom—the Kingdom of Light. This kingdom is also called "the Kingdom of God's dear Son" because the Lord Jesus reigns in this kingdom.

Now we come to one of the most amazing truths in the whole Bible: When Christ passed out of Satan's Kingdom of Darkness and into the Kingdom of Light, He took us with Him!

Yes, that's right! God put us IN CHRIST on the cross. When Christ died, we died with Him.

**The Kingdom of God's Son**

We entered the kingdom of God's Son by our resurrection with Christ.

We passed out of the kingdom of darkness by our death with Christ.

SIN

**The Kingdom of Darkness**

Buried with Christ

When He was buried, we were buried with Him. When He rose again, we rose with Him. We are no longer in the Kingdom of Darkness where sin reigns. We are in "the Kingdom of God's dear Son."

By our death, burial, and resurrection with Christ, we have been delivered from the Kingdom of Darkness and placed in the Kingdom of God's Son. The Bible says, "Giving thanks unto the Father...Who hath delivered us from the power of darkness, and hath translated us into the kingdom of His dear Son."

What does this mean to us? It means that, in Christ, we have been delivered from Satan's Kingdom of Darkness. Sin is no longer our master. Christ is our new Master.

Does this mean that now we cannot sin? No, it does not. As long as we are in this life, we can sin, but we don't have to. We can say "No!" to sin.

God has delivered us from Satan's Kingdom of Darkness. But there are two things we must do to have victory in our lives:

1. We must count on the fact that, in Christ, we died to sin. The Bible says, "Reckon ye also yourselves to be dead indeed unto sin, but alive unto God through Jesus Christ our Lord." To "reckon" means "to count upon the fact."

2. We must choose not to sin. The Bible says, "Let not sin therefore reign in your mortal body." We must say "No!" to sin.

## TEACH THE CHILD THAT, he is in the Body of Christ.

As soon as one believes in the Lord, he becomes a member of Christ's spiritual body. We, along with all other believers, form the Body of Christ, and the local church is the expression of that Body. The Bible says, "For we, being many, are one body in Christ, and every one members one of another."

These words show us how utterly impossible it is for a believer to be independent of other believers. We must impress upon the child the importance of belonging to and supporting the local church. The Bible says, "Not forsaking the assembling of ourselves together." We must be built up with other believers. Only in the local church can we know God's fulness.

## TEACH THE CHILD TO fully yield his life to the Lord Jesus Christ.

There will be little, if any, victory in the life of a believer until he yields his life to the Lord. The child needs to be taught these three great truths:

1. **We belong to the Lord Jesus**. He purchased us with His own blood. (See 1 Peter 1:18,19 and 1 Corinthians 6:19,20.)

2. **Jesus is our LORD**. "Lord" means "master." We must obey Him. (See Romans 14:9 and Luke 4:46.)

3. **We died with Christ and rose again with Him.**
   We are commanded to present ourselves to
   Him "as those that are alive from the dead."
   (See Romans 6:1-14 and 2 Corinthians 5:14,
   15.)

## TEACH THE CHILD TO abide in Christ.

The Lord Jesus came to live in us to be whatever we need. One of His names is "I AM." He says to us, "I AM your love, I AM your patience, I AM your joy, I AM your strength, I AM your victory. I AM your life—I AM whatever you need."

The Bible tells us to "abide in Christ." This means to obey Him, to depend on Him, and to draw on Him for all we need.

A great man of God, Evan Hopkins once explained this to his little son, Evan. Little Evan had received Christ as his Savior when he was just six years old. His father wanted him to understand what it meant to "abide in Christ."

Calling his son, he took a card and drew a circle on it. Inside were all the things that Christ is to us. Putting the point of his pencil in the center of the circle, he said, "There, son, you see that pencil? I want you to keep in Christ as the pencil is in the circle. Inside you will find everything to make you happy and loving and obedient. But there are a lot of little doors all around the circle, and it is when you go out by any of these doors that you are naughty."

Little Evan was so happy to understand this, and he told others in his own words what he had just heard. He carried the card around so he could explain what it meant to "abide in Christ," and how he was staying in the circle.

# ABIDE in CHRIST

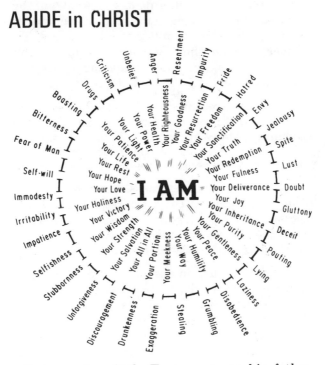

But one day, little Evan came to his father, crying. When his father asked why he was crying, his son said, "I have got out of the circle." He had done something wrong, and he was afraid he could not get back in.

The father knelt with his son, and they looked at the card together. The father said, "Now, Evan, tell me what was the door you went out by?" The son showed it to his father.

"Well," said the father, "the way to get in again is to enter by the same door you went out by. You went out by doing something wrong and the way to get back is to confess that sin to God. The moment you do this, God forgives you of that sin and once again you are abiding in Christ." How happy the little boy was to learn this!

The truths presented in this chapter are sometimes called "the deeper truths," and it is often thought that they are only for older, mature Christians. But children can grasp these truths readily when they are presented in an understandable way.

These victorious life truths are thoroughly explained and illustrated in Courses II and III of The Mailbox Club lessons. We suggest that you study the lessons yourself and use them in teaching these truths to the children.

For my own use in summer camps, I have redrawn many of the diagrams on poster paper using a large, felt-tip pen. The charts have been invaluable in getting these concepts across to the children. Although the material in the lessons is copyrighted, the reader is free to reproduce the drawings in chart form for his individual use.

# Part Three

## The Person God Uses

"It is a mistake to measure spirituality merely by the presence of gifts. By themselves they are an inadequate basis for a man's lasting usefulness to God. They may be present and they may be valuable, but the Spirit's object is something far greater— *to form Christ in us through the working of the Cross*. His goal is to see Christ inwrought in believers. So it is not merely that a man does certain things or speaks certain words, but that he is a certain kind of man. He himself *is* what he preaches. Too many want to preach without being the thing themselves, but in the long run it is *what we are*, and not simply what we do or say, that matters to God and the difference lies in the formation of Christ within...Not gifts but the working of the Cross: this is the measure of a man's spiritual stature."

Watchman Nee
*What Shall This Man Do?*
*(pages 118, 124)*

**How marvelous is the Cross!**

It is the foundation of all that God does *for* the believer, *in* the believer, and *through* the believer.

Note:

In this section we will be using the "Cross" to signify the entire redemptive work of Christ and our union with Him in all of this.

# 15

# THE TEACHER
# Needs Victory Too!

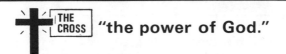 **"the power of God."**

The story is told of a young soldier out on his first night patrol in enemy territory. Soon he called back to his leader, "Captain, I have captured an enemy soldier."

"Good," replied the captain. "Bring him in."

There was a slight pause and then the word came back, "He won't come."

"Well, come on back yourself," shouted the captain.

This time there was a long pause. Then came the plaintive reply, "I can't. He won't let me."

If we are honest with ourselves, most of us would have to admit that our experience regarding Christian victory is often similar to that of the young soldier. Instead of being conquerors, we find ourselves conquered by the world, the flesh, and the devil. And we certainly cannot teach victory to children if we don't know it in our own life.

Has God provided victory over sin, over self,

over the world, and the devil? Yes, He has! He has provided all of this in the Cross of Jesus Christ.

> **The Cross is "the power of God,"** not only for salvation, but also for victory. To have this victory, we must know the deeper meanings of the Cross.

The Bible teaches that God deals with the human race on the basis of two men—Adam and Christ. By our natural birth, we are all IN ADAM. When we are born again by the Spirit of God, we are IN CHRIST.

To be IN ADAM means to share in all that Adam was and all that he did. Likewise, to be IN CHRIST means to share in all that Christ is and all that He did.

Adam was the first man, the head of the human family. When he disobeyed God, he brought the entire human race into Satan's Kingdom of Darkness and under the power of sin. Adam also passed his sinful nature on to his children and to the whole human family.

Jesus Christ is God's Second Man. (See 1 Corinthians 15:47.) He came to deliver us from the power of sin.

To do this, Christ became one with us. He took our place and bore our sins on the cross. He died and was buried, but He rose again the third day as the Head of a new family—the family of God.

Romans 6 reveals one of the most amazing truths in the entire Bible. Not only did Christ die for us but we also died with Him. The Bible says, "Knowing this, that our old man was crucified with Him...that we should no longer serve sin."

# Two Great Facts

CHRIST DIED <u>for</u> us

We Died <u>With</u> Him

God put us IN CHRIST on the cross. When He died, we died with Him; when He was buried, we were buried with Him; and when He rose again, we rose with Him. God's entire work is done, not in us, but in Christ. We share in it because we are IN CHRIST.

We have been delivered from Satan's Kingdom of Darkness by our death and resurrection with Christ. This is a great fact, true of all believers.

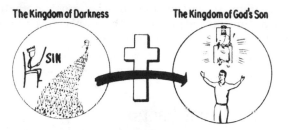

Through the Cross, God has provided victory over all our enemies. When we speak of "the Cross," we mean Christ's death, His resurrection, and His exaltation—and our union with Him in all of this.

### has delivered us from sin's dominion.

The believer is not told to "overcome sin." Instead, he is told to count on the fact that, in Christ, He died to sin.

We are no longer in the Kingdom of Darkness where sin reigns. We are in the Kingdom of God's dear Son. Christ is our Master now, not sin.

These great facts call for faith on our part. The Bible says, "Reckon ye also yourselves to be dead indeed unto sin, but alive unto God through Jesus Christ our Lord."

To "reckon" means "to count upon the fact." God tells us to count upon the fact that, in Christ, we have died to sin's power. This text is one of God's great imperatives. To know its power, we must obey it. James McConkey said, "It is obedience to a command, not the understanding of a mystery, that brings it into the realm of our experience."

> We must reckon, reckon, reckon;
> We must reckon rather than feel.
> Let us be true to the reckoning,
> and God will make it real.–A. B. Simpson

## THE CROSS has delivered us from Satan's world system.

Through the Cross, we can know deliverance from a life of bondage to the things of earth. Through our death with Christ, we have been delivered from "the world." Paul said, "God forbid that I should glory, save in the cross of our Lord Jesus Christ, by whom the world is crucified unto me, and I unto the world."

> Child of the eternal Father,
> Bride of the eternal Son,
> Dwelling-place of God the Spirit,
> Thus with Christ made ever one;
>
> Dowered with joy above the angels,
> Nearest to His throne,
> They, the ministers attending
> His beloved one.
>
> Granted all my heart's desire,
> All things made my own;
> Feared by all the powers of evil,
> Fearing God alone;

Walking with the Lord in glory,
Through the courts divine,
Queen within the royal palace,
Christ forever mine;

Say, poor worldling, can it be,
that my heart should envy thee?

— Ter Steegan

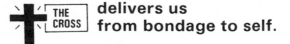 **THE CROSS delivers us from the power of "the flesh."**

The Bible says, "They that are Christ's have crucified the flesh, with the affections and lusts." Those who know their union with Christ can walk in liberty, with no fleshly desires having mastery over them.

**THE CROSS delivers us from bondage to self.**

Self is the root and cause of our sins and failures. As long as we love ourselves more than we love the Lord, we will never know victory in our life. F. J. Huegel said, "Until Christ works out in you an inner crucifixion that sets you free from self-infatuation and unites you to God in a deep union of love, a thousand heavens could not give you peace."

The glory and genius of the Cross is that it disposes us to die to self. Thus the Cross delivers us from bondage to self. The Bible says, "He died for all, that those who live should no longer live for themselves, but for Him who died for them and rose again."

 **is central in victory over Satan.**

At Calvary, the Lord Jesus Christ defeated Satan and all the powers of darkness. The Bible says, "Having spoiled (disarmed) principalities and powers, He made a show of them openly, triumphing over them in it."

It was "through death" that Christ took away Satan's authority and disarmed him. The Bible says that Christ took upon Himself flesh and blood that "through death He might destroy him that had the power of death, that is, the devil; and deliver them who through fear of death were all their lifetime subject to bondage."

> **Faith in our standing**
> **makes it real in our experience.**

How marvelous is the Cross! It is the foundation of all that God does for the believer, in the believer, and through the believer.

Jessie Penn-Lewis, whose writings have been a blessing to so many people, said,

> Believers who know these aspects of the Cross find themselves standing on the solid foundation of the finished work of Christ, so that all Hell cannot shake or overthrow them. They are on the rock-ground of His finished work at Calvary, comprising not only complete atonement Godward, but victory and deliverance from the world, the flesh, and the devil. Even though subjectively it may not be wrought out in their experience in all its fulness, they rely upon all its completeness as theirs...*Their faith is in what Christ has done, not in their experience of it.*

We cannot afford to be ignorant of what God has done for us. We must have a full-orbed understanding of the Cross. We must know what Christ has accomplished for us and our participation in it.

> "There is nothing that the Cross does not separate us from, and there is nothing that the life of Christ is not sufficient for." —James C. Richardson

These great truths cannot be grasped with just casual reading. We must allow the Holy Spirit to burn them into our hearts. We must spend time with God reading and re-reading such books as *The Centrality of the Cross* and *The Cross of Calvary,* by Jessie Penn-Lewis, and the writings of A. W. Tozer, L. E. Maxwell, F. J. Huegel, Watchman Nee, and other Cross-enamored saints.

If we are serious about winning children to Christ, there will be—indeed, there must be—a determination on our part to enter into all that Christ has purchased for us at such infinite cost.

In view of the desperate plight of the children and of the world in general, we cannot afford to live lukewarm, defeated lives. Whatever the cost, we must be willing to pay it.

> **"The people that do know their God shall be strong, and do exploits."**
> *Daniel 9:32*

# 16

# Victorious WARFARE

**"Behold, I give you authority...over all the power of the enemy..."** *Luke 10:19*

Winning children to Christ involves warfare! Satan holds all unsaved people—children as well as adults—in his power, and he does not let his captives go without a fight. The Apostle John wrote, "The whole world lies in the power of the wicked one." Such a statement may shock us, but it is true.

E. V. Thompson, co-founder of West Indies Mission—now WORLDTEAM, said, "Two orders exist in the world today, two kingdoms are locked in mortal combat. And when you are on the cutting edge of God's redemptive work, you are thrust right into the midst of the battle."

How did Satan gain the rulership of this world? Let us review briefly some facts concerning the warfare between God and Satan:

First:     God created this earth. It belongs to Him. (Psalm 24:1)

Second:   God gave the rulership of this earth to Adam. (Genesis 1:26)

Third:    Adam disobeyed God. In doing so, he took sides with Satan, and came under Satan's power. Thus, Adam lost the rulership of the world, and Satan took it over. (Romans 5:12-21)

It is plainly taught in the Scriptures that Satan has the kingdoms of the world under his control. In the temptation of Jesus in the wilderness, Satan took Jesus up into a high mountain and showed Him all the kingdoms of the world in a moment of time. Satan said to Jesus, "All this power will I give Thee, and the glory of them: for that is delivered unto me; and to whomsoever I will, I give it. If Thou therefore will worship me, all shall be Thine." (Luke 4:5-7) Jesus did not deny Satan's claim to the kingdoms of this world.

Fourth:   God wanted to bring this world back to Himself, and He wanted to do it through a man. God sent His Son into the world as His "Second Man." (1 Corinthians 15:47)

Fifth:    A great battle raged between Satan and the Lord Jesus, but Jesus was victorious over all the temptations of Satan. (Luke 4:1-14)

Sixth:    In desperation, Satan stirred up people to crucify Jesus. When Jesus lay in the tomb, Satan no doubt thought he had won the victory. But, on the third day, Jesus arose—Victor over Satan and all the powers of darkness. The Bible says that "through death," Christ rendered powerless "him that had the power of death, that is, the devil." (Hebrews 2:14)

Seventh: The Lord Jesus Christ has been given all authority in Heaven and in earth. Satan and the powers of darkness were stripped of their authority at Calvary. Satan is a defeated foe! (Matthew 28:18, Colossians 2:15, Hebrews 2:14).

Though Satan has been defeated, he has not yet been cast into the lake of fire. For the time being, Satan is free, and he is working as hard as ever to keep unsaved people under his power.

If we are to set the captives free, we must reckon with Satan. Jesus said, "How can one enter into a strong man's house, and spoil his goods, except he first bind the strong man?"

Satan is the "strong man," and unsaved people are his "goods." The Lord is here instructing us concerning a vital principle of spiritual warfare. We must "bind the strong man" before we can "spoil his goods."

The Lord Jesus has defeated Satan. Now God has a work for us to do. We are to enforce Christ's victory of Calvary. God wants us to love people enough to fight for them. Our work is two-fold:

(1) we must "bind Satan," and

(2) we must set his captives free.

**"Behold, I have given you authority...
over all the power of the enemy..."**

*Jesus Christ*

First, we must "bind Satan" by claiming the victory of Calvary in believing prayer—"All that Calvary means, Lord! All that Calvary means!"

The battle with Satan is a spiritual battle and must be fought with spiritual weapons. The victory is won in the secret place of prayer.

Satan does not fear us, but he fears our prayers if we are in touch with God. Why? Because, when we pray, the Lord takes over the battle for us. (See 2 Chronicles chapter 20.)

Before any children's meeting, we should get alone with God and claim the victory of Calvary. The Bible says, "Lift up thy hands toward Him for the life of thy young children." When we have won the victory in the secret place, we can go in the confidence that God is with us.

> In conscious weakness,
>    In the midst of conflict,
> Facing mighty foes,
>    Faith shouts the victor's song,
> "The Lord Himself
>    doth fight for you."

Second, we must "set the captives free" by proclaiming the gospel in the power of the Holy Spirit. This will involve preparation, hard work, and plenty of "stick-to-it-iveness."

> **"Thus saith the Lord, Even the captives of the mighty shall be taken away, and the prey of the terrible shall be delivered: for I will contend with him that contendeth with thee, and I WILL SAVE THY CHILDREN."**
>
> *Isaiah 49:25*

# 17

# POWER
# for Service

"Ye shall receive power, after that the
Holy Ghost is come upon you."

Acts 1:8

It is possible to give the gospel to children
and yet see little results. The message of the Cross
is indeed "the power of God," but its effectiveness depends on whether or not the message is
given in the power of the Holy Spirit.

There is an enduement of power for service
which every believer should know for effectiveness
in God's work. The Lord Jesus intends that our
life shall be the counterpart of His. First, there
is "Bethlehem"—the Son of God coming to live
in our heart. Next, there is "Calvary"—our union
with Christ in His death on the cross. Then "Pentecost"—the power of the Holy Spirit coming upon
us in order that we may witness effectively.

When it comes to our experience, may we always remember that "Calvary" comes before "Pentecost." We must know our death with Christ before we can know the mighty power of the Holy
Spirit in our life. Jessie Penn-Lewis said,

It is because believers seek their share of

"Pentecost" without the deep bedrock work of the Cross and the Resurrection first wrought in them, that the devil as an angel of light has broken in on believers with his counterfeits...The majority of Christians look upon the Cross only as a place for the forgiveness of sins, where they get right with God. Then they cry for a "Pentecostal" enduement, without first asking for a deep work of the Spirit, in the old Adam life being nailed to the Cross, and rendered inoperative. *This is the only safe basic position for an enduement of power.*

God looks not at how much we do, but rather at why we do it and the power we draw upon. If our secret motive is to bring praise to ourselves, the Holy Spirit will stand aside in grieved silence. And if we are using only human ability and talent, our work will have no lasting spiritual value.

The Apostle Paul is our example of a true servant of God. In his epistles to the churches, Paul has told us what he preached, how he preached, and what power he depended on.

## • What Paul Preached

Paul gloried in the Cross. He declared that "the word," or message, of the Cross is "the power of God."

The word translated "power" here is the Greek word "dunamis" from which we get our word "dynamite." It means "power in action." Paul is saying here that the message of the Cross is God's power in action. It has omnipotence behind it!

The message of the Cross is not a favorite theme with most of the wise and cultured of this world, but it is the favorite theme of the Holy Spirit. And it is the message that brings eternal life to those who are lost.

When Paul came to Corinth, he found a city which was highly cultured but sunk in sin. The Corinthians were occupied with learning and philosophy, and they gloried in human wisdom.

No doubt Paul was tempted to use a more intellectual approach here in order to win a hearing for the gospel. He could have done this—he had been educated in one of the finest universities, he had one of the greatest minds in the world, and he knew the Jewish law. Added to all of this, he was a Roman citizen with all the prestige that went with Roman citizenship.

Paul knew that the message of the Cross would be considered foolishness to these educated, cultured Greeks. With all of these considerations, he set aside all "the weapons of the flesh," and preached the simple message of a crucified and risen Savior. Paul said, "For I determined not to know any thing among you, save Jesus Christ, and Him crucified."

## • How Paul Preached

Paul said that he preached the Gospel "not with wisdom of words, lest the cross of Christ should be made of none effect." What a solemn thought—

that the message of the Cross can be made of no effect by the messenger!

John Wesley once wrote to a preacher who had strayed from simple, plain preaching: "I hope you have now got quit of your queer, arch expressions in preaching, and that you speak as plain and dull as one of us." It is not necessary that we be "plain and dull," but flowery oratory is out of place in the message of the Cross.

## • The Power Paul used

Paul depended upon the Holy Spirit to make the gospel effective in the hearts and lives of his listeners. Paul said, "I was with you in weakness, and in fear, and in much trembling. And my speech and my preaching was not with enticing words of man's wisdom, but in demonstration of the Spirit and of power: that your faith should not stand in the wisdom of men, but in the power of God."

We who serve the Lord must understand that there are two kinds of power upon which we can draw—natural power and spiritual power.

Natural power, also called "fleshly power" or "soulish power," is that which comes from ourself, and not from the Holy Spirit. Natural power includes our talents, our knowledge, our gifts, and our personal magnetism.

Natural gifts and abilities can be very impressive, but they cannot transmit God's life to others. "The soul has no carrying power in the spiritual realm. The greatest peril to us in Christian service is to lean upon ourselves, and to draw upon our soul power—our talents, gifts, knowledge, magnetism, eloquence, or cleverness." (Watchman Nee)

True spiritual power is the power of the Holy Spirit. The Holy Spirit alone can give spiritual life to others. The Lord Jesus said, "It is the Spirit who gives life; the flesh profits nothing."

> **The crucified Savior must have "crucified" servants. God does not give his power to "uncrucified" people.**

The Holy Spirit always works on the basis of the Cross. His power is always rooted in the death of Christ. This truth is brought out in the consecration of the priests in the Old Testament.

The Old Testament priests were consecrated by first applying the blood of the sacrifice—a type of our union with Christ in His death, and then applying the oil—a type of the Holy Spirit. The oil was applied only where the blood had been applied. God said, "Upon man's flesh shall it not be poured."

The spiritual principle taught here is that we must know the Cross in our life if we are to experience the power of the Holy Spirit in our ministry. Paul said, "That I may know Him, and the power of His resurrection...being made conformable unto His death."

Because we live in a world that glories in "beautiful people" and TV personalities, it is easy for us to think that one must have great talents and a dynamic personality in order to be effective in God's work. But this is not God's way. God chooses and uses "the foolish, the weak, the base, and the despised."

Jessie Penn-Lewis said, "There is always some danger about the 'wonderful' in believers because it is liable to be attached to the person. It is so much better that we look 'ordinary'...and very insignificent in our lack of visible 'power' while God does His silent working through us in grain of wheat fruitfulness. Then no glory will ever be attached to us, and our personality called 'wonderful.'"

God is not looking for "wonderful" people. He uses ordinary people who have given themselves to Christ—people who are willing to be used and willing to pay the price. Hudson Taylor said, "All of God's giants have been weak men who did great things because they counted on God's being with them." The omnipotent, almighty God with all His infinite resources stands ready to help us.

"O that I may be
    FOOLISH enough to depend upon Him for
        wisdom,
    WEAK enough to be empowered with His
        might,
    BASE enough to have no honor but God's
        honor;
    DESPISED enough to be kept in the dust at
        His feet;
    NOTHING enough for God to be everything."

# 18

# THE SECRET OF
# **Fruitfulness**

"Except a corn of wheat fall into
the ground and die, it abideth
alone..." *John 12:24*

God expects Christians to reproduce themselves
by winning others to Christ. Jesus said, "Ye have
not chosen me, but I have chosen you, and ordained you, that you should go and bring forth
fruit, and that your fruit should remain."

Fruitfulness is one thing; "busyness" is another.
I know someone who used to pray, "Lord, save
us from barren busyness."

Jesus laid down the unalterable law of fruitfulness when He said, "Except a corn of wheat fall
into the ground and die, it abideth alone: but if it
die, it bringeth forth much fruit."

The law of the universe is sacrifice. When you
look at a fruitful field of grain, you are looking at
a vast graveyard. At the root of every fruitful
stalk, a grain of wheat has died.

When a single grain of wheat falls into the
ground and dies, it is raised up to produce many
grains. What has happened to the life of the single
grain? It is now in the many grains. And, as those

grains go down into death, they in turn produce many more grains. Through this process, in just two years, 32,500 grains of wheat can be produced from a single grain! And each grain will possess the life and nature of the original grain.

Jesus was God's precious, perfect "corn of wheat." God said of Him, "This is my beloved Son, in whom I am well pleased." It is God's desire that He have many sons and daughters just like His beloved Son.

How could Jesus reproduce Himself in others? Only by dying. There was no other way. Hudson Taylor, the founder of China Inland Mission, said, "We know how the Lord Jesus became fruitful, not by bearing His cross merely, but by dying on it. Do we know much fellowship with Him in this? There are not two Christs—an easy-going one for easy-going Christians, and a suffering, toiling one for exceptional believers. There is only one Christ. Are you willing to abide in Him, and thus to bear much fruit?"

> There is no gain but by a loss,
> You cannot save but by a cross.
> The corn of wheat to multiply,
> Must fall into the ground and die.
> Wherever you ripe fields behold,
> Waving to God their sheaves of gold,
> Be sure some corn of wheat has died,
> Some soul has there been crucified,
> Someone has wrestled, wept, and prayed,
> And fought hell's legions undismayed.

Recently I heard a missionary tell of his experience on an island off the coast of South America. It was a most difficult field. The people were steeped in a false religion and did not want to hear about Christ.

One man called him aside one day and said, "Let me tell you—go home! You're wasting your time here." People even spit in his face.

That sort of reception could discourage anyone! This brother said, "I've quit a thousand times. I've walked the floor and said, 'Lord, I'm going home!' But the Holy Spirit just said, 'Stay with Me.'" And stay he did.

What is it that causes a gifted, educated man to bury himself in such a place? Nothing less than a Holy Spirit-given determination that Christ shall have the souls for whom He died.

Now, after 23 years, there are seven churches, nine pastors, and over seven hundred believers on that island! What is this? It is simply the Lord's "corn of wheat program" in operation. Of all the plans for producing fruit, none is more certain of success than Christ's own plan—becoming a "corn of wheat" and "dying."

"He saved others; himself he cannot save!" These mocking words were hurled at Christ as He hung on the cross. Mocking words indeed, but they express the law of fruitfulness. Christ could not have saved others if He had saved Himself. And you and I cannot save others if we save ourselves.

Jesus put the matter before us very plainly. He

said, "For whosoever will save his life shall lose it (the fruits of it in eternity): but whosoever will lose his life for My sake, the same shall save it (the fruits of it for eternity)."

Are you willing to be "planted" in the place of God's choosing and to labor there, without any recognition or praise of men, in order that you might bring forth fruit unto God?

The place where God "plants" you is up to Him. It could be some place overseas, and it could be right where you are now. The important thing is that you consecrate your life to the Lord Jesus totally and without reservation.

---

"There is no limit to what God can do through a man who doesn't care who gets the glory."

---

James McConkey's writings have blessed untold thousands of Christians. In one place he tells of his personal, inner struggle over surrendering his life to God. As he wrestled with this matter, the Holy Spirit brought to mind a sentence he had heard in a message—"You can trust the Man who died for you." This turned the tide. He said to himself, "Why, of course, I can trust the Man who died for me."

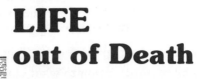

# 19

# LIFE
# out of Death

"So then
death worketh in us,
but life in you."

*2 Corinthians 4:12*

When Gandhi visited England, he was intensely interested in Christianity. He watched those who bore the name of Christ for evidences of supernatural power in their lives. Returning to India, he said, "I greatly admire the Christians' Christ, but I cannot recommend Him to my people, for the majority of His disciples are so unlike Him."

What a tragedy! This man Gandhi, who influenced India as perhaps no other man has ever done, turned away from Christ because of what he saw in the lives of those who professed to be Christ's followers.

We may well wonder how many "Gandhis" we have turned away from the Savior by our unchristlike lives. May the Lord have mercy on us!

We must face the fact that when people touch us—our self-life—they touch death. When they touch Christ in us, they touch life.

**Fruit is not so much
the result of a message,
but rather the outflow of a life.**

Watchman Nee said, "Be assured that the Lord pays far more attention to what comes out of your inner life than what comes out of your mouth. The Lord is not so concerned with your teachings or sermons as He is with the impression you give. What is it that comes out of you—that is the final yardstick. Do you impress people with yourself or with the Lord? Do you let people touch your teachings or your Lord?"[5] We must abide in the death of Christ lest people touch us instead of the Lord.

Every believer has Christ's life within him, and Christ's life is powerful and life-giving. But we hinder His life from going out to others or else we contaminate it with our self-life.

Jesus said, "Abide in Me, and I in you." (John 15:4) Abiding in Christ means many things, but one thing it surely means is to abide in His death. The Lord Jesus says to us, "If you abide in My death, I will live out My life in you."

To come back to Jesus' illustration of the corn of wheat, we know that the life is in the grain of wheat. But there is a very hard shell on the outside. As long as that outer shell is intact—not split open—the life on the inside cannot come forth. Jesus said, "Except a corn of wheat fall into the ground and die, it abideth alone: but if it die, it bringeth forth much fruit."

What happens when the seed goes down into "death"? The darkness, the moisture, and the temperature in the soil combine to crack open the outer shell. Once the shell is split open, the life of the wheat can come forth to produce fruit.

> **It is "dying" and not "doing" that produces spiritual fruit.**

We must be broken by the Lord if Christ's life is to flow through us to others. We must die to our self-love, our self-will, our self-ambition, and all the other thousand forms of self. Our one desire must be that Jesus Christ be glorified and not us. Professor Denney said, "No man can bear witness to Christ and to himself at the same time. No man can give at once the impression that he himself is clever and Christ mighty to save."

> Naught of self to mar His glory,
> Naught of sin to make it dim,
> But a glorious, glorious shining,
> That friends around may see HIM!

The seed not only goes down into death, but it abides there. The new life sinks its roots deeper and deeper into "death." in order that it might grow upward in resurrection life and power.

So it is with us. We must abide in Christ's death if we are to manifest His life. Paul said, "Always bearing about in the body the dying of the Lord Jesus, that the life also of Jesus might be made manifest in our body."

Why must we always bear about in the body "the dying of the Lord Jesus"? Because when people touch our self-life, they touch death. Our self-life must be continually dealt with by the Cross in order that Christ's life may flow out to others.

We say, "Christ is the answer," and He is. But the Cross is needed to make a way for Him. We have to make a way for the living Christ by abiding in His death. If we do this, He will surely manifest His life through us. Paul said, "We which live are always delivered unto death for Jesus' sake, that the life also of Jesus might be made manifest in our mortal flesh. So then death worketh in us, but life in you."

In her book, *The Centrality of the Cross,* Jessie Penn-Lewis tells of how she came to learn the secret of fruitfulness. She was enjoying a happy, glorious experience with the Lord when she came across a book by Madam Guyon. This book set forth the message of the Cross and the way of fruitfulness. Mrs. Penn-Lewis wrote:

> As I read the book, I clearly saw the way of the Cross, and all that it would mean. At first I flung the book away and said, "No, I will not go that path."

> But the next day I picked it up again, and the Lord whispered so gently, "If you want deep life and unbroken communion with God, this is the way." I thought, "Shall I? No!" And again I put the book away.

The third day I again picked it up. Once more the Lord spoke, "If you want fruit, this is the path. I will not take the conscious joy from you; you may keep it if you like; but it is either that for yourself, or this and fruit. Which will you have?"

And then, by His grace, I said, "I choose the path for fruitfulness," and every bit of conscious experience closed. I walked for a time in such complete darkness—the darkness of faith—that it seemed almost as if God did not exist. And again, by His grace, I said, "Yes, I have only got what I agreed to," and on I went.

I did not know what the outcome of this would be, until I went to take some meetings, and then I saw the fruit...From that hour I understood, and knew, intelligently, that it was dying, not doing, that produced spiritual fruit.

**The secret of a fruitful life is—in brief— to pour out to others and want nothing for yourself: to leave yourself utterly in the hands of God and not care what happens to you.**

# 20

# God Wants to Use YOU!!!

"The eyes of the Lord run to
and fro throughout the whole
earth, to show Himself
strong in the behalf of them
whose heart is perfect
toward Him." *2 Chronicles 16:9*

A large portion of this book is devoted to
methods. These methods have been tried and proven, but their success depends on the person using
them.

> If the person himself is not right, no
> method will be successful.

In his book, *Power Through Prayer*, E.M.
Bounds says, "The trend of this day has the
tendency to lose sight of the man or sink the man
in the plan or organization. God's plan is to make
much of the man, far more than anything else.
Men are God's methods."

"The Church is looking for better
methods; God is looking for better
men."

We don't have to beg God to use us. He wants to use us. The thing we must ask ourselves is: Am I usable? Vance Havner put it bluntly: "If God isn't using you, it's because you are not usable."

How do we make ourselves usable? We make ourselves usable by allowing God to work into us the qualities He wants in His workers. We are going to consider some of these qualities by asking ourselves some questions. As you answer these questions for yourself, keep in mind that God *wants* to use you.

## FUNDAMENTALS

Some qualities are absolutely essential to a life of effectiveness and fruitfulness in God's service. Even though we know about them, we need to be reminded of these qualitites from time to time.

### • Do I have assurance of my salvation?

Strange as it may seem, it is possible to know and even to preach that Christ died for the sins of every person in the world, and yet somehow not realize that He died for your sins.

John Wesley, the founder of Methodism, came to this country and spent three years as a missionary. Then, in Georgia, he met a Moravian preacher who spoke to him about his own salvation. After his return to England, John Wesley wrote in his journal, "What have I learned? Why, I have learned what I least of all suspected, that I, who went to America to convert others, was never myself converted to God." Soon after this, John Wesley came to a real assurance of his salvation.

## • **Am I totally consecrated to Christ?**

Until you give yourself totally to Christ, you will not have God's power upon your life. L.E. Maxwell, founder of Prairie Bible Institute, said, "Your power with God will be in direct proportion to your enslavement to Christ."

In the sacrifices of the Old Testament, there was the "sin offering" which represented Christ's atoning death for us. There was also the "burnt offering" which represented our giving ourselves to God for His service.

Various sacrifices were acceptable for the burnt offering. A wealthy man could offer an ox; a man of lesser means could offer a lamb; and a poor man could offer a dove. All of these offerings were equally acceptable to God. But, in each instance, it was the offering of a life— a total life.

This is what God expects of us—the offering of our total life. In our case, God does not ask for a dead sacrifice but a "living sacrifice." Paul wrote, "I beseech you therefore, brethren, by the mercies of God, that you present your bodies a living sacrifice, holy, acceptable unto God, which is your reasonable service."

Since the Lord bought us with His own precious blood and we belong to Him, it is most reasonable that we should give Him His property.

> "If Jesus Christ be God, and He died for
> me, then no sacrifice is too great for me
> to make for Him."   *C. T. Studd*

"Will you tell me in a word what consecration is?" asked a student. Holding out a blank sheet of paper, the teacher replied, "It is to sign your name at the bottom and let God fill it in as He chooses."

## • Am I separated from worldliness?

A Christian is a "Christ-one," and whatever is inconsistent with our relationship to the Lord must be rejected. Wilbur Chapman said, "Anything that dims my vision of Christ, or cramps my prayer life, or makes Christian work difficult, is wrong for me, and I must, as a Christian, turn from it."

God's Word says plainly, "Know ye not that the friendship of the world is enmity with God? Whosoever therefore will be a friend of the world is the enemy of God."

I shall never forget a statement made by my spiritual counselor, Paul LaBotz. He said, "You can go where the people of this world go, and you can do the things they do, but you won't have any power with God."

## • Is there any unconfessed or unforsaken sin in my life?

God is very loving and patient with His

children, but He is never soft on sin. He says that He will not hear our prayers if we are holding on to some sin in our life. (Psalm 66:18)

> **"Jesus Christ has no tenderness whatever toward anything that is ultimately going to ruin a man in the service of God."** *Oswald Chambers*

## • Am I abiding in Christ?

The Lord Jesus explained our relationship to Him with a simple but profound illustration from nature. He said, "I am the vine, you are the branches." Just as the branch cannot bear fruit unless it abides in the vine, so we cannot bear fruit unless we abide in Christ. Jesus said, "Without me you can do nothing."

To abide in Christ means to trust Him, to obey Him, and to draw upon Him for all your needs. You may be a new Christian and know very little about the Bible; yet you can abide in Christ and bear fruit for Him. Jesus said, "He that abideth in me, and I in him, the same bringeth forth much fruit."

## RELATIONSHIPS

All believers are members of the Body of Christ, and, as such, they are dependent upon one another. The Bible says, "As we have many members in one body...so we, being many, are one body in Christ, and every one members one of another."

God never meant for us to go it alone. His plan

is that we work together with other believers to accomplish what we could never do alone. For this reason it is essential that we be in right relationship with the other members of the Body.

## • Do I handle offenses according to God's Word?

Life being what it is, we will always have problems, offenses, and "personality conflicts." But it is a serious thing to hold a grudge against someone.

In Matthew 18, the Lord Jesus tells us what to do if someone has offended us. We are not to talk to other people about it, but we are to go to the person who offended us, tell him of his offense and make things right.

In Matthew 5, the Lord tells us what to do if we have offended someone. We are to go to that person and ask his forgiveness.

> "I will not permit any man to narrow and degrade my soul by making me hate him." *Booker T. Washington*

To allow bitterness and unforgiveness to take root in our heart and to poison our spirit is tragic and inexcusable. God simply cannot use a person who has a bitter, unforgiving spirit. But how blessed it is when God's people are noble and magnanimous in their dealings with others.

John Wesley and George Whitefield represented two widely differing schools of theology. They had both private and public differences. Though both men were God-anointed leaders, their strife was long and heated. But in time the breach was healed, and Whitefield and Wesley became the best of friends. Whitefield even requested John Wesley to preach his funeral service.

Upon Whitefield's death, Wesley honored this request. After the funeral, a lady approached John Wesley and asked, "Mr. Wesley, do you expect to see dear Mr. Whitefield in heaven?"

"No, madam," was Wesley's immediate reply.

Somewhat taken back, the lady answered, "Ah, I was afraid you would say so."

"Do not misunderstand me," said Wesley. "George Whitefield was so bright a star in the firmament of God's glory, and will stand so near to the throne, that one like me, who am less than the least, will never catch a glimpse of him."

## • Do I get along with other Christians?

A brother once said jokingly, "I sure would enjoy Christian work if I just didn't have to work with people." Well, of course! But that's what Christian work is—working with people.

> To live above with the saints we love,
> Oh, that will be glory!
> But to live below with the saints we know,
> Well, that's a different story!

In God's work, everything depends upon His blessing. If God does not bless our work, we will be like those disciples of Jesus who said, "We have fished all night and caught nothing."

1. He drew a circle to shut me out.

2. Rebel! Heretic! a thing to flout!

3. But love and I had a wit to win.

4. We drew a circle that took him in!

Edwin Markam

God's blessing is invariably found where His children work together in love and harmony. "Behold, how good and how pleasant it is for brethren to dwell together in unity...for there the Lord commanded the blessing."

## PRACTICAL CHRISTIAN LIVING

A Christian worker is just that—a worker. Some might think that "spiritual service" for the Lord gets done by saying, "Fill my cup, Lord." But it is more than this. It involves preparation, discipline, hard work, and perseverance.

As Christians, we must all one day stand before our Lord to give an account of what we did with our lives after we were saved. To avoid embarrassment then, it is important that we check up on ourselves now.

### • Am I preparing myself so God can use me?

When I asked a man of godly wisdom how I could better serve God, he replied, "Get your tools ready and God will use you."

"How do I get my tools ready?" I asked.

"Memorize Scripture! Memorize Scripture!" was his answer.

 Every time you memorize a portion of God's Word, you are equipping yourself with another tool to use in serving God.

To be an effective Christian worker, you *must* acquire a grasp of the Word of God. The Bible says, "Study to show thyself approved unto

God, a workman that needeth not to be ashamed, rightly dividing the word of truth."

Anyone who says that he wants to serve God and yet is not willing to take time to study God's Word cannot expect God to take him seriously.

## • Am I diligent?

Many Christians are asking for God's blessing, but they are not working in a way that will bring His blessing. The Holy Spirit simply will not bless what we do carelessly and half-heartedly. The Bible says, "Cursed be he that doeth the work of the Lord negligently."

Serving God carries with it an obligation to do things in a way that will glorify Him. Some workers assume that because they are "in the Lord's work," they can be excused for careless preparation, shoddy materials, and half-hearted work. Anyone who thinks that God is pleased with such work simply does not know God.

> The only place where "success" comes before "work" is in a dictionary!

## • Are my priorities right?

Before we become Christians, we can run our lives as we want to. But, once we become Christians, our life-long duty is to serve God.

God does not require that every Christian lay aside his job and preach the gospel full-time, but He does require that we be totally consecrated to Him. Whatever work you may be doing, once you become a Christian, your first priority is serving God. All other jobs become side lines.

A Christian businessman in Chicago had it right. When someone asked him what his business was, he replied, "My business is winning people to Christ. I pack pork to pay expenses."

## • Do I stick to the work God has given me to do?

D.L. Moody, the founder of Moody Bible Institute, said that the secret of accomplishing something for God is *consecration*—the giving of our all to God, and *concentration*—the devoting of our all to the work God gives us to do.

The Lord appreciates stick-to-it-iveness on the part of His servants. The Apostle Paul said, "This one thing I do." Better to say that than, "These fifty things I dabble at."

> **Remember, a diamond is just a piece of coal that stuck with it!**

## • Am I disciplined?

The world is full of brilliant people who have never achieved a fraction of what they are capable of doing. Why? Because they do not discipline themselves. John Wesley believed in sanctification by faith, but He also got up every morning at 4 o'clock to spend time with God in prayer and Bible study.

Among other things, discipline means mastering your moods so that you do what you should do, whether you feel like it or not.

When a college student explained to his professor that he skipped his last class because he just didn't feel like it, the professor roared back, "Young man, has it ever occurred to you that most of the work done in this world is done by people who don't feel like it?"

## • Am I serious-minded?

In speaking to children about salvation, we must impress on them that salvation is a most serious matter. If we are not serious, how can we expect them to take us seriously?

Life is serious, death is serious, hell is serious, Satan is serious, the Holy Spirit is serious, and we must be serious too.

## FELLOWSHIP WITH GOD

The Christian life is a life of fellowship with God. It was said of Enoch that he "walked with God." As we consider some of the essentials of a life of fellowship with God, may it be our heart's desire and purpose to walk with God.

## • Have I settled all controversies with God?

Many believers fail to go on with God because they have a controversy with Him. Usually God deals with us about one matter at a time. We may agree with Him on a hundred other matters, but He always brings us back to this particular issue.

We may as well face the fact that we will make no progress whatever in our Christian life until we say "Yes" to God on this matter. Sometimes it takes God ten, fifteen, twenty or more years to bring a child of His to the point of agreeing with Him.

We cannot afford to waste our lives like this. If we are not honestly willing to do what God wants us to do, at least we can say to Him, "Lord, though I am not willing to do this, yet I am willing for You to make me willing." If we are sincere in this prayer, God will begin working to change our hearts.

## • Do I love the Lord Jesus?

Trying to serve Christ without loving Him is like being married to someone without loving them. The heart of the relationship is missing.

Jesus Christ loves us passionately, and He wants us to love Him passionately. The secret of an effective witness is a warm, personal, overflowing love for the Lord Jesus.

## • Do I have a daily Quiet Time with the Lord?

One of the greatest mistakes a Christian can ever make is to let work and activities crowd out time with God. Each day we must spend time alone with God in prayer and in the study of His Word.

A daily Quiet Time is not some deluxe option in the Christian life—something you can take or leave according to your personal preference. It is absolutely essential if you want your life to count. S.D. Gordon wrote:

A life of victory hinges on three things: an initial act, a fixed purpose, and a daily habit. The initial act is that of personal surrender to the Lord Jesus as Master. The fixed purpose is that of doing what will please Him and only that, at every turn, in every matter, regardless of the consequences. The daily habit is that of spending a quiet time in prayer alone with the Lord over His Word. After the initial act of surrender, the secret of a strong, winsome Christian life is in spending time daily alone with God over His Word in prayer.

## WILL YOU LET GOD USE YOU?

Someone reading this may think, "I fall so short of what God wants me to be. I don't see how God can use me." Don't be discouraged! God is not looking for "perfect" instruments. He is looking for "willing" ones.

**"Don't worry if you feel weak. That's a prerequisite for accomplishing things."**
*Dawson Trotman*

By far the most important thing is your heart attitude. If your heart attitude is to love God and to do His will, He will use you.

Once there was a young man who fell into sin and was dying of tuberculosis. An elderly servant of God preached the gospel to him, telling him how the Lord Jesus had borne all his sins, and urging him to repent, confess his sins, and receive the Lord to be his Savior.

At first this youth felt quite reluctant, being obsessed with the thought of how ever could God forgive such a sinner as he. Yet finally he did accept the Lord and was saved. He felt so happy and peaceful. After a few days the elderly servant of God revisited him, finding his face full of grief and pain. So he asked the young believer: "Why are you so sad? Do not let Satan deceive you!"

He answered, "I know my sins have been forgiven."

"Then why are you so sad?"

Forlornly he answered, "My days on earth are quite finished. What can I bring to the Lord when I shall stand before Him? My hands are empty. Must I go and see the Lord empty-handed?" Such was the reason for his grief.

The elderly man comforted him by saying, "Brother, do not be discouraged. I will

use your words to write a song. And who-
ever is constrained by this song to go
abroad to preach the gospel and win souls,
you shall have the reward." Now this was
the song that Charles C. Luther wrote
which has since become famous: "Must I
Go and Empty-handed? Must I Meet My
Savior So?"

Many have been aroused by this song
and have fervently served the Lord. Although this young man had lost many of
his days, he still retained a little heart
desire for the Lord at his dying, and the
Lord fulfilled it.[6]

Oh, the joy of leading a soul to Christ! D. L.
Moody said, "I believe that if an angel were to
wing his way from earth up to Heaven, and were
to say that there was one poor, ragged boy, without father or mother, with no one to care for him
and teach him the way of life; and if God were to
ask who among them were willing to come down
to this earth and live here for fifty years and lead
that one to Jesus Christ, every angel in Heaven
would volunteer to go."

But God has not given this privilege to angels.
He has given it to us. Perhaps you are a new
Christian and you wonder what you can do. Do
not think that you must wait many years before
you can serve the Lord. You can serve Him now.

You may be a busy housewife, but you can find
time to tell children of the Savior's love. Invite
them to a little party at your house and share

with them what Christ has done for you. Children love to hear about personal experiences.

You may be an older person and your heart aches as you think of the opportunities that have gone by and the years you have wasted. Do not be discouraged. God says, "I will restore to you the years that the locust has eaten."

An 80-year-old grandmother wrote to tell us of the joy she had found in sending Bible correspondence lessons to children and how this had filled a void in her life. She said, "When my grandson was saved through the lessons, this was all I needed to make my cup run over."

Whether you are younger or older, don't let your work or some other activity crowd out God's interests. We all need to be reminded that we have "Only one life; 'twill soon be past. Only what's done for Christ will last."

To enter Heaven and see our Savior face-to-face ...that will be JOY. But to bring many precious boys and girls with us...that will be JOY MULTIPLIED!

When I enter that
Beautiful City,
And the saints all
around me appear,
I hope that someone
will tell me,
"Hey, it was YOU
who invited me here!

*Corrie Ten Boom*

**Important!
You have not finished
reading this book until you
complete the next pages.**

# How to *Get Going!*

This book has been written with the burden that your heart will be challenged to win children to Christ. The essential information needed to get started has been presented, but information requires response.

To help you get started, we have added this Work Sheet. Complete it with care.

**You are doing business with God.**

## WORK SHEET

Since it is important that you write down your thoughts and decisions, space is provided right in this book. However, you may wish to use a separate piece of paper. Pray, think and then write.

## 1. Am I willing to let God use me?.......Yes ☐ No ☐

We trust that your answer is "Yes," but if not, list the reasons why you are not willing. Then take the list to the Lord with the prayer, "Lord, I am willing to be made willing. I will overcome these obstacles with Your help."

_____

_____

_____

_____

_____

_____

## 2. Am I willing to establish a Daily Quiet Time? . . . . . . Yes ☐ No ☐

**I will begin a Quiet Time by (date)** _____

(If you checked "No," proceed as in #1.)

_____

_____

_____

_____

_____

## 3. Am I willing to take some definite steps to enable me to win children to Christ?
### Yes ☐ No ☐

List each step and the date to take the step. In a third column note the date that the step was actually taken or begun. (If your answer is "No," proceed as in #1.)

| THE STEP | TAKE BY (date) | ACTUALLY TAKEN (date) |
|---|---|---|
| | | |
| | | |
| | | |
| | | |
| | | |
| | | |
| | | |

**4.** In my present circumstances, I believe the best way(s) for me to serve God is by: (List present opportunities or possible opportunities.)

_____

_____

_____

_____

_____

I will endeavor to begin by (date) _____

After you have done all that you can do on the Work Sheet, go to the next page.

## DO NOT READ THIS PAGE
## Until you have finished
## the "GET GOING" work sheet.

After you have exhausted your own
creative thinking on your Work
Sheet, here are further ideas which
may be of help.

## 1. Am I willing to let God use me?

Some people are unwilling to commit themselves to God because they are not sure of
what He might ask them to do. God reveals
His will to willing hearts. If we *will* to do His
will, then God will show us what He wants us
to do. (See John 7:17.) And remember, God
*wants* to use you. (Phil. 2:13.)

## 2. Am I willing to establish a
## Quiet Time?

In order to have a fruitful and a continuing
Quiet Time, you must work out some sort of
system. You may wish to write one of the
following for daily devotional or Bible study
materials: Navigators, Radio Bible Class or
Bible Pathway. Addresses are given under
Resource Materials.

## 3. Am I willing to take some
## definite steps?

Here are some steps that you might take:

1. Enroll in your church's evangelism training
   programs.

2. If there is a Child Evangelism Fellowship chapter in your area, enroll in the training program.

3. Memorize Scripture. It would be helpful to enroll in a Scripture Memorization program. Write Navigators or Bible Memory Association.

4. Send for materials mentioned in this book.

## 4. In my present circumstances, I believe that the best way(s) for me to serve God is:

Here are some suggestions:

1. Teach a Sunday school class.

2. Get involved in your church's visitation program.

3. Start a children's Bible club in your home. Or begin by helping someone else with a Bible club.

4. Invite children to your church and see that they have a way to get there.

5. Use Bible correspondence lessons to hand to children or mail to them.

We trust that the Work Sheet and these suggestions will get you going.

## Do something

## and do it NOW!

> "Now therefore perform the doing of it; that as there was a readiness to will, so there may be a performance..."
>
> *2 Corinthians 8:11*

## God Bless You!

# Believe on the Lord Jesus Christ

Avis B. Christiansen, b. 1895

Harry D. Clarke, b. 1888

1. "What must I do?" the trem-bling jail - or cried, When dazed by
2. What must I do! O wea - ry, trem-bling soul, Just turn to-
3. His blood is all thy plea for sav - ing grace, The pre - cious

fear and won - der; "Be - lieve on Christ!" was all that Paul re - plied,
day to Je - sus; He will re - ceive, for - give and make thee whole —
fount of cleans-ing! O come, ac - cept His love, be - hold His face,

**REFRAIN**

"And thou shalt be saved from sin." Be - lieve on the
Christ a - lone can set thee free.
And be saved for - ev - er - more. Be - lieve

Lord Je - sus Christ, Be - lieve on the Lord Je - sus Christ, Be-
Be - lieve

lieve on the Lord Je - sus Christ, And thou shalt be saved!
Be - lieve

## ACKNOWLEDGEMENTS

1. *Handbook of Child Evangelism*  Copyright © 1955 by Child Evangelism Fellowship Inc. All rights reserved. Used by permission.

2. Adapted from *A Story Your Hand Wants to Tell You* Copyright © 1963 by Wayne Leitch. Used by permission.

3. Sketches from *Wordless Book Visualized.* Copyright © 1950 by Child Evangelism Fellowship Inc. Used by permission.

4. *Evan Hopkins* by Alexander Smellie. Published by Marshall Bros., Ltd. London.

5. *John Wesley* by Basil Miller. Published by Bethany Fellowship, Inc. Minneapolis, Minn. Used by permission.

6. *Boy Wanted*, edited by L. E. Maxwell.  Published by Prairie Bible Institute, Three Hills, Alberta, Canada.

7. *The Release of the Spirit* by Watchman Nee  Copyright © 1965 The Sure Foundation. Used by permission.

8. *The Practical Issues of Life* by Watchman Nee  Copyright © 1975 Christian Fellowship Publishers, Inc. Used by permission.

# Scripture References

# Scripture References

# RESOURCE MATERIALS

### BIBLE MEMORY SYSTEMS . . .

The Navigators/NAVPRESS
P.O. Box 35001, Colorado Springs, CO 80935
(800)366-7788

Bible Memory Association
P.O. Box 12000, Ringgold, LA 71068-2000

### BIBLE STUDY HELPS . . .

Bible Pathways
P.O. Box 1515, Murfreesboro, TN 37133

Radio Bible Class
Box 22, Grand Rapids, MI 49555

Moody Center for External Studies
820 N. LaSalle Boulevard, Chicago, IL 60610-3284

Back to the Bible Broadcast
Box 82808, Lincoln, Nebraska 65801

### DEEPER LIFE BOOKS . . . Write:
Christian Literature Crusade,
P.O. Box 1449, Fort Washington, PA 19034

### CHILDREN'S CHURCH MANUALS . . . Used in conjunction
with Visualized Bible Lessons (see below). Each manual provides
five month's curriculum. Order from:
Bible Visuals, Inc., P.O. Box 153, Akron, PA 17501-0153

### CHILDREN'S LESSONS, STORIES, SONGS, etc . . .

Child Evangelism Fellowship Press
P.O. Box 348, Warrenton, MO 63383

Bible Visuals, Inc.
P.O. Box 153, Akron, PA 17501-0153

### TODAY'S CHILD . . . Excellent magazine written for those who
are teaching and evangelizing children. Order from your local CEF
director or write: TODAY'S CHILD, Warrenton, MO 63383.

### MAILBOX CLUB LESSONS . . . Bible correspondence lessons
for all ages. Special Introductory Kit contains all lessons and

materials for 10 students. Three different age levels. Full instructions included in each kit. $11.95 postpaid. Order from: The Mailbox Club, 404 Eager Road, Valdosta, GA 31602.

**VISUALIZED BIBLE LESSONS . . .** A series of illustrated Bible lessons which teach Bible doctrine in simple, understandable language. Excellent for teachers of children, teens, and adults. Order from: Bible Visuals, Inc., P.O. Box 153, Akron, PA 17501-0153. Also: CEF Press, P.O. Box 348, Warrenton, MO 63383.

**WORDLESS BOOK MATERIALS . . .**

The Wordless Book Visualized -- flash card edition. Ring binder. Scenes are printed in the book. Does not require use of flannel board. Inexpensive and easy to use. Not as effective as the flannel board but good to start with.

**ON CASSETTE . . .** The Wordless Book message used effectively in thousands of children's meetings. By author George B. Eager. Recorded live. $4.95.

Wordless Book materials may be obtained from: The Mailbox Club, 404 Eager Road, Valdosta, GA 31602.

# RECOMMENDED READING

"Nothing sets the heart on fire like truth."

(Address of publisher given only at first mention of publisher.)

ABIDE IN CHRIST, Andrew Murray (Christian Literature Crusade, Fort Washington, PA 19034). A thirty-one chapter devotional study based on John 15. To thirsty souls this book can open up an entirely new and blessed experience in fellowship and communion with Christ.

BONE OF HIS BONE, F.J. Huegel (Zondervan, 1415 Lake Drive, Grand Rapids, MI. 49506). The central theme is that we are to see in the cross of Christ not only expiation, but also identification.

BORN CRUCIFIED, L. E. Maxwell (Moody Press, 820 N. LaSalle St., Chicago, IL 60610). A vital study of the believer's identification with Christ in His death and resurrection. Very readable.

CENTRALITY OF THE CROSS, THE, Jessie Penn-Lewis (Christian Literature Crusade). Excellent studies on the centrality of the cross in the believer's victory over sin, the world, the flesh, and the devil.

CROSS OF CALVARY, THE, Jessie Penn-Lewis (Christian Literature Crusade). A full-orbed study on the meaning and message of the cross. Meditating on these studies will enrich any believer's life.

GOD'S WORD MADE PLAIN, Mrs. Paul (Kay) Friederichsen (Moody Press). An excellent, bird's-eye course on what the Bible teaches. Many valuable pictorial illustrations.

INDOMITABLE MR. O, THE, Norman Rohrer (Child Evangelism Fellowship Press, Warrenton, MO. 63383). The amazing story of the struggles, testings, and ultimate triumph of the man who founded the world's largest evangelistic outreach to children.

KNOWLEDGE OF THE HOLY, THE, A. .W. Tozer, (Harper and Row, Scranton, PA. 18512). One of the best books ever written on the attributes of God. Every believer should read this at least once a year.

NORMAL CHRISTIAN LIFE, THE, Watchman Nee (Tyndale House Publishers, Box 80, Wheaton, IL 60189). A Christian Classic setting forth in clear, understandable language the truths of the believer's union with Christ and the way of victory.

PURSUT OF GOD, THE, A. W. Tozer (Christian Publications, 25 South Tenth Street, Harrisburg, PA. 17101). A deeply spiritual book for every believer who hungers to know God.

SIT, WALK, STAND, Watchman Nee (Tyndaly House Publishers). The spiritual position, walk, and warfare of the Christian as set forth in Ephesians. Very readable.

TEACHING THE WORD OF TRUTH. Donald Grey Barnhouse (Wm. B. Eerdmans Publishing Co., Grand Rapids, MI. 49502). One of the best books available on teaching God's Word. Christian teachers around the world have used this book with its simple teaching methods and illustrations to convey to young Christians of all ages the truths of the Scriptures.

THREE-FOLD SECRET OF THE HOLY SPIRIT, THE, James H. McConkey (Back To The Bible Broadcast, Box 82802, Lincoln, NE. 68501). A study of the incoming, fulness, and manifestation of the Holy Spirit by a most gifted Bible teacher. This is one of the simplest and clearest books available on this subject. Over five hundred thousand copies have been printed.

# what is the **MAILBOX CLUB ?**

The Mailbox Club is a Bible correspondence club which can be enjoyed by people of all ages.

Bible lessons are sent through the mail to members. Through these lessons they learn the great truths of the Bible.

## Who can have a MAILBOX CLUB?

Any believer! Our plan is so simple that any born-again Christian who loves the Lord and loves children can do it... at home!

## What do I do?

You mail or give a lesson to the student. The student fills out the answer sheet and sends it back to you. You grade it and send the next lesson.

## Does it Work?

YES! Thousands are coming to know Christ each year through these lessons. Over 5 million Mailbox Club lessons are printed annually.

**See and Do** for 4,5,6 and 7 year-olds.

**Storytime** for 7 and 8 year-olds.

**Explorer's** for 9,10 and 11 year-olds.

**Course A** for 12,13 and 14 year-olds.

**Love, Dating and Marriage** for teens and young adults.

**Course 1** for teens and adults.

**New Life in Christ Course 1** for teens and adults.

**New Life in Christ Courses 2 and 3** follow New Life-1.

**Practical Christian Living** for teens and adults.

| Extra Large Print | **The Way to Heaven** for adults. In extra large type for easy reading. |
|---|---|

# It's Easy To Start
# A Mailbox Club!

**1. Get lessons and materials** from The Mailbox Club. An Introductory Packet is good because it contains samples of all materials used.

**2. Put your name and address in two places** on every lesson before sending it out.

 Your RETURN ADDRESS here on the address side.

 Your address here so that the answer sheet can be mailed back to you.

If you have many lessons to do, have a rubber stamp made of your address. Lettering should be large enough to read easily.

**3. Give or mail the proper lesson 1** to the student. (See opposite page.) The student reads the lesson, fills out the answer page and mails it back to you.

**4. Grade the lesson.** Study the lessons yourself so that you understand them well and know the exact answers as found in the lesson. Encourage your students with a little note on each answer sheet.

**5. Mail graded answer sheet** back to the student along with the next lesson.

**6. Keep records** of each student's progress. We have file cards for records.

(Complete set of instructions sent with each order of an Introductory Packet)

*177*

# From our Book Department:

### • *The Way to Heaven*

This book tells you how you can be sure that you are going to Heaven. Answers so many questions about the Bible and the way of salvation. Tells you how to study the Bible.

**176 pages--Paperback $5.00**

### • *New Life Discipleship Series*

This 13-week study course explains simply and clearly why every person needs to be born again and how to experience the new birth. Daily Bible readings and a devotional guide help the student into a happy, fruitful walk with the Lord. Ideal for small group study. **160 pages-- Spiral bound $5.95**

*"The New Life series is a 'must' for every new Christian and fantastic for the serious student of the Bible."* --Dr. Stan Craig

### • *Love, Dating and Sex:  What Teens want to know*

Especially written for junior high and high school teens.  Tells teens why they should say **NO** to sex before marriage and **how** to say **NO**. Every young person should read this book! Short chapters, superb art, true-life stories.

After hearing the principles taught in this book, a 17-year-old boy wrote, *"I have been involved in many sexual relationships because I did not know the facts.  Now that I do [know the facts], I refute sex before marriage."*

This would make a great gift for any pre-teen or teen.  Order several copies!  **208 pages--Paperback $9.95**

### • *Love, Dating and Marriage*

For teens and singles. Gives Biblical principles on love, dating and marriage in plain, understandable language. Loaded with truelife stories that young people can identify with and learn from. **160 pages--Paperback  $5.95**

*"I've been in the ministry 30 years and this book, Love, Dating and Marriage, is the best. "*
-- G.N., pastor, Ary, KY.

# Book Order Form

| How Many | Item | Unit Price | Total |
|---|---|---|---|
| | Winning Children | 5.95 | |
| | The Way to Heaven | 5.00 | |
| | New Life Discipleship | 5.95 | |
| | Love, Dating and Sex | 9.95 | |
| | Love, Dating and Marriage | 5.95 | |

| | | |
|---|---|---|
| Total | | |
| Add for shipping | | |
| TOTAL ENCLOSED | | |

### Please Print

Name _____

Address _____

City _____ City _____ Zip _____

| Add for shipping: | Orders of $1.00 to $10.00 | $2.50 |
|---|---|---|
| | $10.01 to $25 | $3.50 |
| | Over $25 | $4.50 |
| | Overseas: Pay in U.S. Funds and add 20% for shipping. | |

Enclose Payment and
Mail Your Order To:

**MAILBOX CLUB BOOKS**
404 EAGER ROAD
VALDOSTA, GA 31602

*PAYMENT MUST ACCOMPANY ORDER.*